VAASTU

SECRETS FOR A BETTER LIFE

Dr Puneet Chawla

Vaastu Secrets for a Better Life

First Edition 2008

Published by
Ravi Dhariwal for the proprietors,
Bennett, Coleman & Co. Ltd.,
New Delhi

ISBN	: 978-81-89906-25-2
Editorial	: Monali Banerjee
Design	: Subhasish Munshi, Balkishan Verma, Ashwani Madan
Illustration	: Jitender Kumar
Marketing Team	: Ajay Bansal, Raj Verma
Printed And Bound By	: Nutech Photolithographers
Price	: Rs. 200

CONTENTS

PREFACE

Let's face it. We all want to live a life of comfort and peace, and in a disease-free and tension-free environment. And there's nothing wrong with wanting it. From the humblest living being walking this Earth to the most advanced being — man — each and every one of us want to live in comfortable environs, and in tranquility. To ensure a peaceful existence, it is imperative to live within a secure and well-balanced structure, and this is where Vaastu Shastra comes in. So what exactly is Vaastu? Based on certain age-old principles, Vaastu is a science which enhances the quality of life by harmonizing the five elements which are a must for survival: Water, Air, Earth, Space and Fire. Along with these five elements, Vaastu — which developed in the fifth and sixth centuries — lays down specific rules and regulations as to the design and architecture of a structure, based on the energy lines running through the Earth. Once positive energies and vibrations have been developed, these have to be maintained — Vaastu Shastra lays down some dos by which this is possible — and only then will balance and harmony reign in our lives. Through *Vaastu Secrets for a Better Life,* Dr Puneet Chawla tells us how we can achieve this much-needed harmony in our lives. A Vaastu expert, Dr Chawla has transformed many lives by analysing and then rectifying the Vaastu defects within a particular structure, bringing a sea change in the lives of his clients. A dearth of easy-to-understand books on Vaastu has motivated him to pen this book.

Written in a reader-friendly style — with tips galore — *Vaastu Secrets for a Better Life* has been categorized into three sections, which have been further subdivided into chapters which deal with ideas that are relevant to that particular section.

In "Introduction to Vaastu", the meaning of Vaastu and what it entails for mankind, the Vaastu Purush and Vaastu Mandala have been discussed in the first chapter of the book, while the importance of directions in creating a harmonious environment in homes, has been dealt with in the second chapter. The Five Elements of Earth, Space, Air, Fire and Water, and the Subtle Energies, and the Symbols of Vaastu, which are again essential for a Vaastu-friendly environment, have been discussed in the third and fourth chapters.

In the next section, "Vaastu at Home & in the Workplace", selection of plots, Vaastu for structures, placing of the main entrance to the house, and various other rooms in the house have been discussed with simple tips to eliminate confusion and dos and don'ts that will reduce, if not totally remove, negative energies within the house. Chapters 16 and 17 offer tips for harmonizing the workplace, as well as tips for the employer to ensure that business offers keep pouring in and subordinates remain focused in their work. Chapters 18–20 deal with those important constructions in the building which are rarely given their due: stairs, height and elevation, levels and slopes, and water, oil and septic tanks.

In the third section, "Vaastu for Better Living", you'll find tips and suggestions on colour combinations, the right usage of which will enhance positive energies and thoughts in your life. The other chapters in this section offer tips on using Vaastu for improving one's energy levels and quality of life.

Case studies on workplace/factories, residence, kitchens, bedrooms and bathrooms have been included in the Appendix, which throw light on the problems that the families faced and the measures that were taken to remove Vaastu defects.

Thus, as can be seen, Vaastu advises the correct structuring and planning of the house, and rooms within the house, and other commercial buildings as well. The tenets prescribed in Vaastu Shastra can be used by anyone and everyone, so that each one of us can live in harmony and in balance with nature, and subsequently attain our life ambitions, and contribute as responsible and productive citizens of the society, and country.

But it is necessary to remember that Vaastu is not a religion, but a science, and while we can better our life conditions with the help of Vaastu, there is no substitute to integrity and hard work. Vaastu aims at removing the negative energies that limit our potential, and brings back peace in our lives, thereby enabling us to concentrate fully on our work and transform our dreams into reality.

So as you seek to walk ahead on the path charted by your destiny, do try and incorporate the tips given in this book to make your life simpler and tension-free.

WHAT IS VAASTU?

Society is ever-changing. Morals, values and social mores have changed from one period in history to another, but one philosophy has remained constant: the need and desire for money and success. The one who has power commands and receives respect in society. If we consider karma as the seed of our happiness and sorrow, and our destiny as the soil, then our environment (Vaastu) becomes the fertilizer and water for our karma. Therefore, by changing our environment — Vaastu — we can strengthen the chances of success.

SOME DEFINITIONS IN VAASTU

Vaastu stands for balance and a harmonious environment within a structure. This involves balance in all the ten directions of the universe. These directions provide subtle energies which can be sensed, like gravitational energy, solar magnetic energy, airflow, etc. When we build a structure, the flow and availability of all the energies has to be taken care of. If these energies are not harmonious in the structure, Vaastu defects are created and our life becomes difficult. If there is harmony in all energies, we say there is a positive environment and if there is disharmony, we say it has a negative environment.

In simple terms, Vaastu can be called the Science of Architecture. Vaastu Shastra is an ancient art and science with well-defined principles and practices of constructing buildings which ensures a happy balance between man and nature, thereby bringing all-round happiness, health, wealth and prosperity. The break-up of the word "Vaastu" as "Vaas-tu" has a very clear and distinctive meaning: "Vaas" means residence and "Tu" means God, or "the place where God can live"; we can take it one step further, by defining it as "good land for living".

There are several ancient scriptures which speak about Vaastu, but of these the most important ones are: *Raj Vallabh, Somarangam Sutradhar, Aprajita Parichcha, Maya Mattam, Manasara,* and *Kautilya Shastra*. All types of buildings, cities, forts, industries, etc, wherever humans live or work is called Vaastu.

Vaastu involves the orientation of the house to the direction, the dimensions of the structure, space, rooms, allocated floors, bathrooms, kitchens, dining area, design of the main gate, building gate, building elements — depending upon the family, cost involved, and one's own lifestyle. The science of Vaastu Shastra helps one to enjoy the natural benefits offered by the five basic elements of the universe: Sky (*Akash*), Earth (*Prithvi)*, Water (*Jal*), Fire (*Agni*), and Wind (*Vayu)*. Vaastu Shastra can be applied by harnessing and harmonizing these five basic elements of nature.

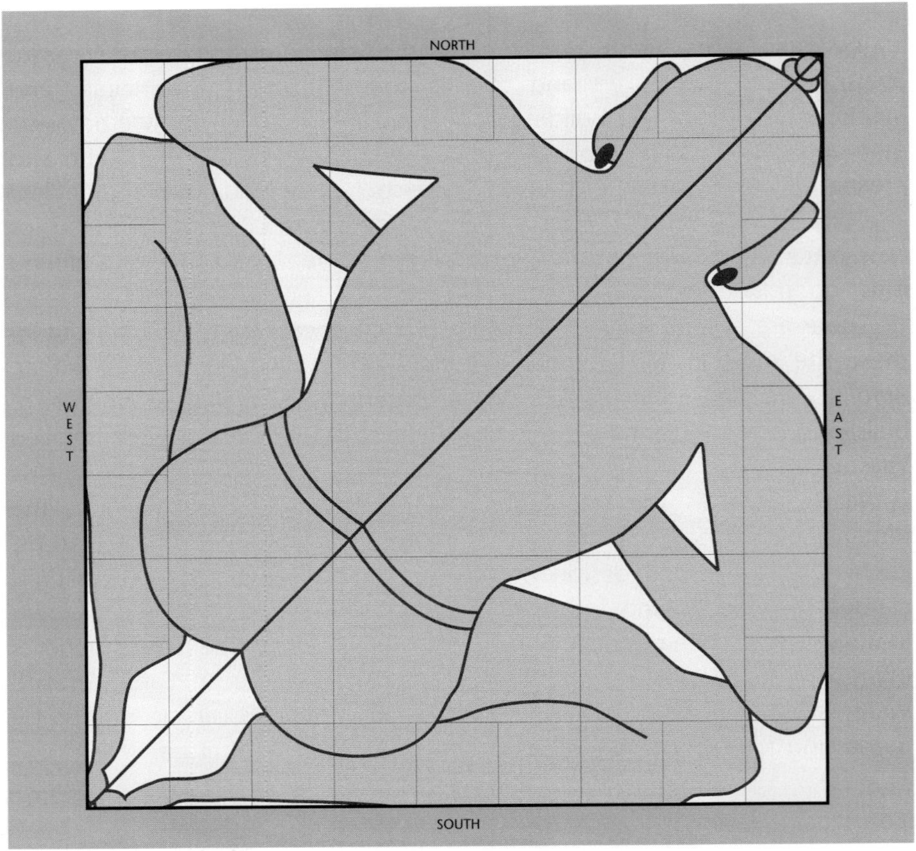
NORTH
WEST
EAST
SOUTH

VAASTU PURUSH

According to a statement in the *Matsya Purana*, as Lord Shiva fought and killed the demon Andhakasur, a drop of his sweat (Lord Shiva's) fell on Earth, and with that sweat, the Vaastu Purush was created.

The Vaastu Purush was extremely cruel and brutal by nature, and ate everything and everybody on his way. This appalled all the deities in Heaven, and under the leadership of Lord Indra, they imprisoned the Vaastu Purush in a square pit in the Earth — with his head in the North-east, and feet in the South-west. And that is the posture in which he lies in every single plot of land.

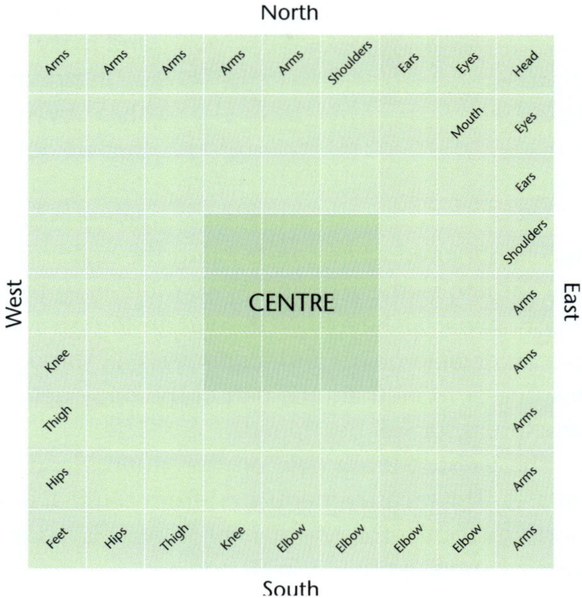

The Vaastu Purush thereafter worshipped Lord Shiva, seeking a boon. Pleased with him, Lord Shiva blessed him that whosoever constructed a building

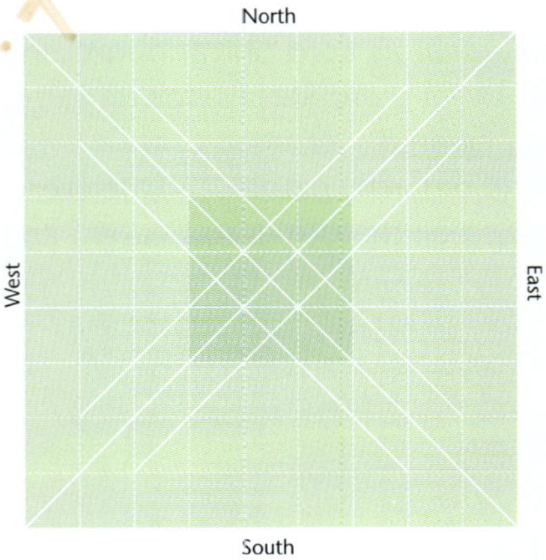

would worship him first, and make offerings to him. In return, the Vaastu Purush would bless the occupants and protect them from any ill fortune. Since then, the Vaastu Purush is called the spirit of the building. To appease him, one must do ceremonies and rituals, and make offerings to satisfy him.

In present life conditions, we must abide by some spiritual rules of life so that we don't harm anyone. The Vaastu Purush has certain *marma* or delicate points in his body, which should not be hurt and injured while constructing the building.

According to the scripture *Maya Mattam* — this should be known to every house owner/architects — the Vaastu Purush has six bones, a single heart, four vulnerable points and four vessels. If, through the architect's ignorance, any one or more than one part of the body gets "injured", the owner of the structure is, or will be, ruined.

The Vaastu Purush, laid on the ground/land, is measured in the form of squares. The measurements start from cardinal directions of East to West and North to South. The Mandala of Squares is made in two forms, one is of 64 squares and the other is in 81 squares.

East

North (left) — South (right)

Shikhi & Diti	Parjanya	Jayant	Indra	Surya	Satya	Brish	Anil & Antriksh
Aditi	Aditi & Parjanya	Jayant	Indra	Surya	Satya	Brish & Pusha	Pusha
Bujang	Bujang	Aapvatsa & Aap	Aryma	Aryma	Savita & Savitra	Vitathat	Vitathat
Som	Som	Prithvidhar	Bhrama	Bhrama	Vivasvan	Brithttakst	Brithttakst
Bhallat	Bhallat	Prithvidhar	Bhrama	Bhrama	Vivasvan	Yama	Yama
Mukhya	Mukhya	Rudra & Rajyashma	Mitra	Mitra	Indra & Yayant	Gandharva	Gandharv
Nag	Shosh & Rudra	Asur	Varun	Pushpadant	Sugriva	Bhringraj & Devarik	Bringhraj
Rog & Papshyama	Shosh	Asur	Varun	Pushpadant	Sugriva	Devarik	Mrig & Pita

West

Diagram Showing 64 squares

East

1 Shikhi	2 Parjanya	3 Jayant	4 Indra	5 Surya	6 Satya	7 Brish	8 Antariksha	9 Anil
32 Diti	33 Aap	Jayant	Indra	Surya	Satya	Brish	34 Savitra	10 Pusha
31 Aditi	Aditi	35 Aapvatsa	Aryma	36 Aryma	Aryma	37 Savita	Vitahth	11 Vitahth
30 Bujang	Bujang	38 Prithvidhar	Bharma	39 Bharma	Bharma	40 Vivasvan	Brithttakst	12 Brithttakst
29 Som	Som	Prithvidhar	Bharma	Bharma	Bharma	Vivasvan	Yama	13 Yama
28 Bhallat	Bhallat	Prithvidhar	Bharma	Bharma	Bharma	Vivasvan	Gandharv	14 Gandharv
27 Mukhya	Mukhya	41 Rajyashama	Mitra	42 Mitra	Mitra	43 Indra	Bringraj	15 Bringraj
26 Nag	45 Rudra	Shosh	Asur	Varun	Pushpadant	Sugriva	45 Jaya	16 Mrig
25 Rog	24 Papyashama	23 Shosh	22 Asur	21 Varun	20 Pushpadant	19 Sugriva	18 Dowairk	17 Pita

North (left side) — South (right side)

West

Diagram Showing 81 squares

Varahamihira's *Brihat Samhita*, mentions that 45 deities occupy the Vaastu Purush's body. These 45 deities are:

1. Shikhi	13. Yama	25. Rog	37. Savita
2. Parjanya	14. Gandharv	26. Nag	38. Prithvidhar
3. Jayant	15. Bringraj	27. Mukhya	39. Bhrama
4. Indra	16. Mrig	28. Bhallat	40. Vivasvan
5. Surya	17. Pita	29. Som	41. Rajyashama
6. Satya	18. Dowairk	30. Bujang	42. Mitra
7. Brish	19. Sugriva	31. Aditi	43. Indra
8. Antariksha	20. Pushpadant	32. Diti	44. Rudra
9. Anil	21. Varun	33. Aap	45. Jaya
10. Pusha	22. Asur	34. Savitra	
11. Vitahth	23. Shos	35. Aapvatsa	
12. Briththtakst	24. Papyashama	36. Aryma	

VAASTU MANDALA

Mandala means configuration, a system which is defined as a network and the common form of the *mandala* is a square field. Energy networks are expressed graphically in the matrix in the form of squares or any other defined shape. The Vaastu Purush Mandala is a square grid and is said to be a fundamental form in which both architecture and other shapes and sizes can be created. This *mandala* is oriented to the four cardinal directions. According to the Vaastu Mandala, 32 deities reside in the four cardinal directions, ie, North, East, West and South. Each direction is divided into nine

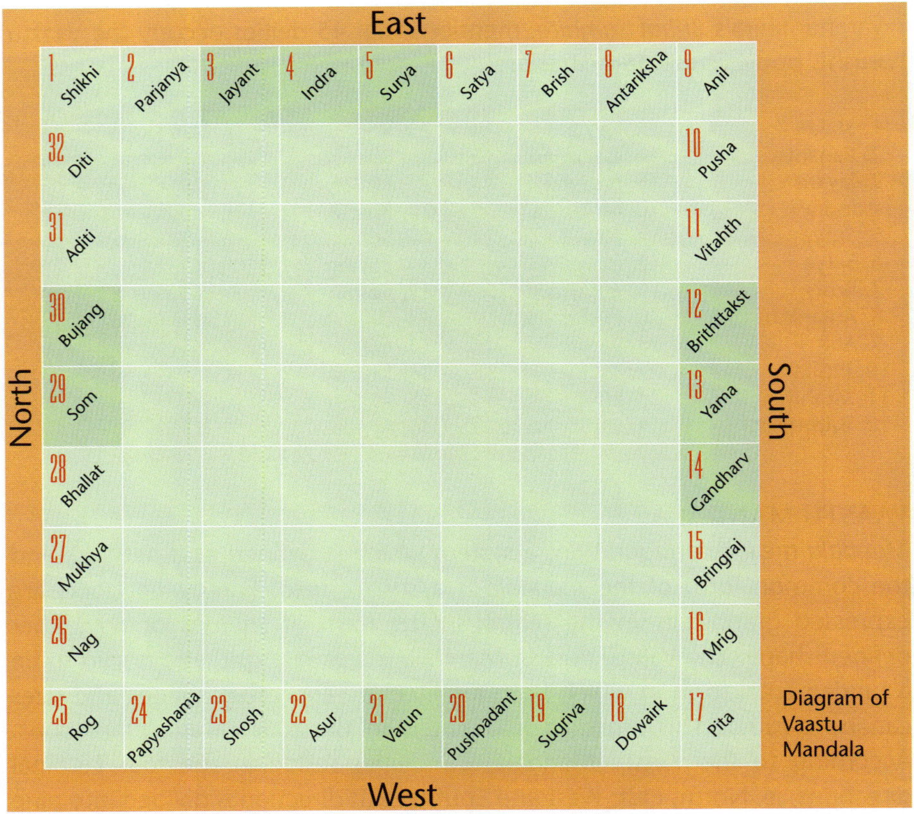

Diagram of Vaastu Mandala

parts, each of which is occupied by a deity.

The *Matsya Purana* states that in a square form, there should be a total of 81 parts, all equal to one another, and 45 deities reside in these 81 parts; out of these 45 deities, 32 reside in the outer squares that make up the boundaries, and 13 in the inner squares of the grid. Every deity has its own good or bad attributes.

One should propitiate these deities and chalk out the building plan, entrances and doors according to the Vaastu Mandala.

EAST

1. The first place is occupied by Lord Shikhi and a main entry here denotes sorrow, loss and fear from fire.

2. The second place is occupied by Lord Parjanya. Placing a door here will certainly invite grief and poverty.

3. The third place is occupied by Lord Jayant. Doors in this place mean that the occupants will be blessed with money.

4. The fourth place is occupied by Lord Indra. Placing the main door here ensures both respect and fame.

5 ▸ The fifth place is occupied by Lord Surya. A door here gives both power and money.

6 ▸ The sixth place is occupied by Lord Satya. A door in this place means both loss and theft.

7 ▸ The seventh place is occupied by Lord Brish. Placing a door here creates both anger and cruelty.

8 ▸ The eighth place is occupied by Lord Antariksha. A door in this place will invite theft and loss from fire.

SOUTH

1 ▸ The ninth place is occupied by Lord Anil, and placing a door here will lead to health problems for the inmates.

2 ▸ The tenth place is occupied by Lord Pusha. A door here will give the occupant a bad name in society.

3 ▸ The eleventh place is occupied by Lord Vitahth, and a door here will cause fear and depression.

4 ▸ The twelfth place is occupied by Lord Brithttakst. A door in this place gives good children and prosperity.

5 ▸ The thirteenth place is occupied by Lord Yama, and a door in this place gives monetary gains.

6 ▸ The fourteenth place is occupied by Lord Gandharv and placing a door in this place makes the occupants fearless.

7 ▸ The fifteenth place is occupied by Lord Bringraj. A door here will cause both poverty and diseases.

8 ▸ The sixteenth place is occupied by Lord Mrig. Doors in this place denote poverty and diseases as well.

WEST

1 ▸ The seventeenth place is occupied by Lord Pita. Placing a door in this region means poverty and enemies.

2 ▸ The eighteenth place is occupied by Lord Dowairk. Women will face a variety of problems if a door is put in this area.

3. The nineteenth place is occupied by Lord Sugriva, and a door in this place gives prosperity to the owner.

4. The twentieth place is occupied by Lord Pushpadant. A door in this place will ensure both monetary gains and a happy and healthy family to the owner.

5. The twenty-first place is occupied by Lord Varundev. Doors in this area bring both money and good luck.

6. The twenty-second place is occupied by Lord Asur and a door in this place signifies bad luck.

7. The twenty-third place is occupied by Lord Shosh. A door here is sure to bring unimaginable loss and bad luck.

8. The twenty-fourth place is owned by Lord Papyashama. Diseases and grief will come to the occupants if a door is placed here.

NORTH

1. The twenty-fifth place is owned by Lord Rog. Doors in this region will cause problems that are tantamount to death and poverty.

2 ▸ The twenty-sixth place is owned by Lord Nag. Enemies, disrespect and bad luck will fall on the occupants if a door is put here.

3 ▸ The twenty-seventh place is owned by Lord Mukhya. The occupants will face loss if a door is placed here.

4 ▸ The twenty-eighth place is occupied by Lord Bhallat. Placing a door in this place ensures both money and abundance. Indeed, this place gives overall abundance.

5 ▸ The twenty-ninth place is occupied by Lord Som. A door in this region gives obedient children, money and prosperity.

6 ▸ The thirtieth place is occupied by Lord Bujang. Disharmony and quarrels within the family will prevail if doors are placed in this area.

7 ▸ The thirty-first place is occupied by Lord Aditi. Occupants will have enemies and face obstructions in life if a door is placed here.

8 ▸ The thirty-second place is occupied by Lord Diti. A door here will bring diseases and obstructions.

BE AS TRUE TO EACH OTHER AS THE DIAL IS TO THE SUN

IMPORTANCE OF DIRECTIONS IN VAASTU

The Science of Vaastu is based essentially on directions. As such, a thorough knowledge of directions and their significance, according to Vaastu, is imperative when constructing a building. Further, to get your Vaastu absolutely right, you have to understand the implications of the East and the West directions.

In olden days, people minutely observed the shadows cast by the sun in order to check directions. Today, however, a magnetic compass is used to confirm directions. While there are ten directions in total, a compass can verify only eight of these.

A compass covers a total of 360 degrees with its radius, with 45 degrees allotted to each of the eight directions. Checking the level of degree within each direction is also an important aspect of Vaastu.

As mentioned above, there are a total of ten directions. The four main directions are North, South, East and West. There are four sub-directions, which comprise the corners. These are:

North-east (Ishan)	Between the North and the East.
South-east (Agneya)	Between the South and the East.
South-west (Nirutya)	Between the South and the West.
North-west (Vayaya)	Between the North and the West.

The remaining two directions are Space (*Udharv*) and Centre.

DIRECTIONS AND THEIR ATTRIBUTES

North

This is one of the most auspicious directions. The owner of this direction is Kuber, Lord of Wealth and Prosperity, which is why the North is known as the wealth and career direction. The planet for this direction is Budh (Mercury).

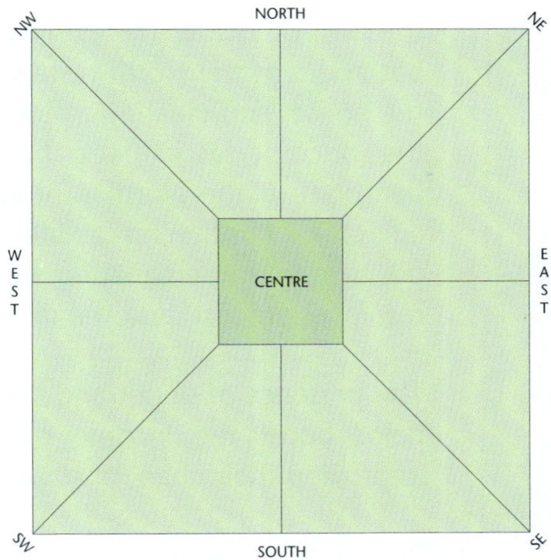

1. The Vaastu Purush's chest occupies the northern direction, and as such, this area should be kept uncluttered, well lit and spacious.

2. Vaastu consultants also believe that the North receives a tremendous amount of positive energy from the North Pole. This energy is extremely beneficial to a structure and is also important for the residents of the building. Keeping this in mind, it is imperative that there should be large openings in the North to help the structure receive these positive energies.

3 ▸ When designing a house, it is essential to ensure that all rooms and facilities are positioned correctly in relation to the North, so as not to harm or hinder the positive effects of this direction. Placing a bathroom in the North results in heavy losses to the occupants of the house, and creating a store here can also lead to stagnation in their income, as it blocks finances. Similarly, placing the master bedroom in the North promotes restlessness and, hence, is not advisable. Positioning a kitchen in this direction burns all the positive energy emanating from the North. As a result, financial resources are lost, and the family falls into debt.

4 ▸ The presence of slopes and underground water tanks in the North helps boost the income of the residents of the house, thus improving their financial status.

5 ▸ Placing large mirrors on the northern wall of a room enhances the benefits provided by this direction. This is because whatever is reflected in the mirror is doubled.

6 ▸ Avoid placing closets on the North walls of the room, as it makes the wall heavy and, in turn, stops the North's energy from flowing freely.

7 ▸ If the number of doors in the North are fewer and smaller in size than the doors in the South, it can create Vaastu defects and lead to expenditure-related problems.

8 ▸ In the case of buildings that face the North, the elevation of the building in the front should not be higher than that of the other sides. This can result in serious Vaastu defects.

South

Although widely considered to be a bad direction, the South is actually not so. The corresponding planet for this direction is Mangal (Mars). The South's negative reputation stems from its owner Yama, Lord of Death. He is also in charge of legal affairs, and so, Vaastu defects in this direction may cause problems arising from legal matters. The South also affects the growth of financial prospects, business and career. However, the South is, in fact, the bank for all the good energies emanating from the North, and it stores this energy in the form of wealth for the house.

1 ▸ To ensure that there is no leakage of these energies, the South should not have any big openings. Closed places in the South are considered prosperous, while large access points in this direction can give rise to problems that are comparable to death.

2 ▸ To further store and stabilize the energies, you can make the South heavy by placing lots of furniture and closets here. It is also a good idea to create a store or granary in this direction, especially for those living in a joint family.

3 ▸ Thick walls in the South keep Yama at bay from the residents of the house.

4 ▸ Avoid placing mirrors on the southern walls of the house as it may enhance and expand the negative features of the South, and may not be good for finances. The same stands true for wall clocks and calendars, which are also not favourable. Instead, hang pictures of large buildings or mountains on these walls, as this will help keep problems at bay and also provide support to the people residing in the building.

5 ▸ It is good to use colours such as red and other dark shades in the southern areas of the house. You can create red interiors, which may include red walls, red curtains, red flowers, etc.

6 ▸ Bedrooms in the South can be given to children or other younger people in the house/family.

7 ▸ The presence of a bore well in the South can cause major problems in a family, and may also lead to huge financial losses.

East

This is a very powerful direction, and is owned by Indra, Lord of Prosperity, Festivity, and Power. He is also a masterful manipulator. The representative planet for this direction is Surya (Sun), a powerful entity in its own right that none can match. The sun supports life and vegetation, and so the East is also known as the direction for growth. As the direction of sunrise, the East stands for prosperity and fulfilment in life because the sun purifies, cleanses and energizes the entire universe.

1 ▸ Like the North, the East should also be kept open, light and clean. Thick walls and absence of windows and doors in this direction results in a lack of ventilation in the house. This can cause stagnation in the lives of the residents. Remember, that any obstruction in the East can create an obstruction in your life. Always keep the East open, ventilated, light and clean. Openings in the East bring in a lot of solar energy, which has therapeutic properties. To reap the benefits of solar energy, let there be maximum openings along the East wall of your house/office. Even the curtains on the windows in the East should be light in both fabric and colour. Use light pastel shades in leaf green and cream on the eastern walls.

2. Building a staircase, a bathroom or store in the East is a major Vaastu offence and can cause many problems. A staircase here may lead to heart-related problems, while a store in the East blocks the flow of energies to the western section of the house. This creates difficulties in growth and prosperity.

3. If a building faces the East, the front courtyard should be kept open and spacious. If the front courtyard has a concrete floor, and the backyard on the West side is not solid, such as a garden, the building's occupants may face problems pertaining to financial growth.

4. The presence of a puja room, study room and conference rooms in the eastern part of a building is considered good. Hanging pictures of deities on the eastern walls of the house is auspicious.

5. A lower level floor in the eastern room is also auspicious, as it brings prosperity and happiness in a family.

6. Try to face the East while working or watching television.

West

This direction is known for bringing stability in life, and is occupied by the lower abdomen, genitals and reproductive organs of the Vaastu Purush. Its owner is Varundev, Lord of Water, Rain, Fame and Fate. The corresponding planet for the West is Shani (Saturn). The West is more powerful at night and gets activated after sunset.

1. As the sun rises from the East and sets in the West, the axis of energy also travels from the East to the West. This energy (solar) from the East cannot be stored in the West if there are large openings in this direction. Therefore, avoid creating access points and entries in the West, as they can harm any prospects of income. If you have to create windows here, make sure they are smaller than those in the East. Western walls should be strong to bar subtle energies from flowing out. The stronger the walls in the West, the happier will you be.

2. Couples should not occupy bedrooms located in the western portion of the house, as it can result in transferable jobs for either of the partners, and the couple will find it difficult to live together for long periods. The bedrooms in this direction can, however, be occupied by children or guests; or leisure rooms, restrooms, and family sit-outs. Washrooms in the western part of your property is a good idea.

3. A kitchen located in the West may give rise to excess expenditure and create instability in income.

4. Similarly, a puja room in this direction is inauspicious, and gives rise to feelings of selfishness and self-centredness among family members.

5. Rainwater-harvesting facilities, bore wells, and water slopes in the western portion of a plot or building is not good. This may create health problems for the menfolk in the family.

6. The West is ideal for positioning overhead water tanks as Lord Varundev, owner of this direction, symbolizes water.

7. Constructing a kitchen in the West is neither prosperous nor pious.

8. Underground water tanks, borings and swimming pools are not considered auspicious if located in the West.

9. Do not make any water storage tanks in the western section of your plot.

10. The West should always be heavier than the East. Plant big trees on the western periphery or make a large mural on the western wall. You can also make it heavy by keeping solid furniture along the western wall.

11 ▸ While selecting a plot, make sure that there are no gardens or open spaces facing the West.

12 ▸ The main gate of your house should never be in the West or even the South-west, for that may bring ill luck to you and your family.

13 ▸ Do not hang mirrors on the western wall. Hang family pictures instead to receive good energies from the East.

14 ▸ Extensions in the West are not good; they create delays in your life.

15 ▸ Use dark shades such as violet and grey on the western walls to suit the dark nature of this direction.

North-east

This is truly a wonderful direction, the benefits of which one can enjoy if used properly. The owner of the North-east is the supreme deity of Hindus, Shiva. The representative planet for the direction is Brihaspati (Jupiter), who bestows knowledge and spiritual growth. The North-east generates an extremely powerful axis of magnetic energy, which travels across to the South-west, and it is known as the main provider of overall prosperity, health and wealth. In my experience, nearly 60 per cent of Vaastu principles lie in this highly pious and sensitive direction.

1. It is essential to keep this corner spacious and free of any obstacles that might obstruct the free flow of energy mentioned above. Avoid building a bedroom, store or any room that would hold heavy furniture in this area. The North-east should be kept as open as possible. This will keep tensions and problems far away from the occupants of the house.

2. It is also equally important to keep the North-east clean. This is a highly sensitive direction, and represents the face of the house. The Vaastu Purush's face also lies in the North-east corner.

3. Make a puja room in the North-east. This is the most pious corner in the house, occupied as it is by Lord Shiva.

4. The North-east symbolizes wisdom and learning, and as such, is a great direction for scholars and students. Hence, this is a good place for placing a study room. The strong energies here improve one's concentration and memory.

5. Positioning a building's main entries in the North-east is believed to be very auspicious.

6. Constructing a toilet in the North-east is a serious Vaastu blunder;

this can cause health problems in a family or result in major losses in business in the case of a commercial organization. Also, avoid placing garbage in this direction.

7. Similarly, avoid placing a garage, transformer or generator, staircase, or a overhead water tank in the North-east. All these elements can create problems for the family. However, you can place an underground water tank here.

8. Placing an element of Fire in this area can cause accidents, as this area belongs to the Water element. Any interaction between these two opposing elements creates havoc within the house. As such, never position a kitchen in this corner — it may lead to clashes between family members and cause health problems for the lady of the house.

9. Couples occupying a North-east bedroom may face health-related problems. Moreover, any conception that has taken place in this room can lead to a miscarriage or create fears regarding the birth of mentally retarded children.

10. Make sure that there are no elevated platforms in the North-east.

This corner emits magnetic energies, and if it is elevated, these energies are suppressed and cannot flow into the house.

11 ▸ A slope heading towards the North-east corner is very good. Since this direction is owned by the Water element, if a slope of water is diverted towards the North-east, prosperity follows the residents of the house. The presence of natural pits in this corner is also very auspicious.

North-west

The owner of this direction is Vayudev, Lord of Wind. The planet of this direction is Chand (Moon). As it is powered by the element of Wind, the North-west is highly unstable. This powerful direction is known for creating opportunities in life, and if used in accordance to Vaastu principles, it can take your career to immense heights. Conversely, the incorrect usage of the North-west results in instability, indecision and diseases. It can also create a sense of restlessness among the residents of the building.

1 ▸ The North-west is a great corner for a guest room or a drawing room. It is also a good location for a finished goods store, as it helps in the quick movement of material and fewer delays in payment.

2 ▸ A master bedroom in the North-west causes instability in the income

of the occupant. Similarly, a study room in this corner results in loss of memory, confusion, and lack of concentration. Students find it difficult to study and spend less time in the study room.

3. The North-west corner should be kept free of any clutter and blockage, especially metals and other junk, as this may cause administrative and legal problems.

4. An elevated floor in the North-west section of a house can cause problems in the higher education of the children.

5. If a married son occupies the North-west room, he is likely to move away from home.

South-east

This direction resembles a well-wisher, who although sensitive, is angry by nature. The owner of the South-east is Agni, Lord of Fire, and its representative planet is Shukra (Venus). The sun, the provider of life to this universe, is at its harshest when it enters this direction, and the heat generated is compared to Fire. Hence, the South-east is always reserved for fire-related devices. Since Fire is highly potent and opposed to elements such as Water and Air, great care should be taken while decorating this area. The use of South-east is a very delicate matter.

1. The South-east is the best location for a kitchen. Since this corner belongs to Lord Agnidev, all food cooked here is blessed by Him and is believed to be very healthy and prosperous.

2. Never place your bedroom in the South-east, as this causes serious Vaastu problems. The ultraviolet rays of the sun reach this direction by noon and accumulate in the South-eastern room throughout the day, making it uncomfortable for the occupants. This can result in behavioral problems for them. Couples may face strained relations, sometimes even leading to divorce.

3. Placing overhead water tanks in the South-east is like creating an enemy in the house. It can lead to lots of unwanted problems related to electrical and electronic equipments. Underground water tanks in this direction are also not good. It may result in unwanted tensions and clashes with family members, relatives and friends. It can cause legal and administrative problems as well.

4. Water slopes heading towards the South-east also bring in problems, as do swimming pools. This can lead to fire-related accidents and other tensions.

5. Placing a *mandir*, puja room or a study room in this area is also not

advisable, as due to its heated environment, it is not considered to be a peaceful location. The same stands true for safes storing cash and important files.

6 Avoid positioning a building's main entries in the South-east as this is very risky, and brings in unforeseen problems for the occupants. It may create legal problems as well.

7 Do not place a mirror in the South-east. This may result in losses for business organizations.

South-west

This direction is owned by a demon called Niriti, and its corresponding planet is Rahu. The South-west is the strongest direction in the plot as it stores magnetic energies flowing in from the North-east. If used properly, this direction can give you a strong and healthy life, confidence, wealth, fame and health. However, incorrect usage of the South-west can result in serious problems for the residents of the structure. These include major losses in finances, emergence of behavioral issues such as depression, anxiety and suicidal feelings, loss of energy at the workplace, and even problems relating to conception within a family.

1 The South-west is the best place for a master bedroom, as one is

always safe and happy in this part of the house. The owner of this bedroom enjoys both good health and wealth. It is also the most restful place in a building. Make sure that the master of the house occupies the bedroom here. If it is given to the son, especially one who is newly married, it may create family problems. Since a South-west bedroom is very strong, with dominating overtones, it can cause clashes between the mother-in-law and daughter-in-law.

2 ▸ Cash and valuables stored in the South-west are stable and long-lasting. As such, it is a good idea to place the cash drawer of a business unit or shop in this corner.

3 ▸ The South-west is the worst place for positioning a building's entry, and should be avoided by all means. An entry here can cause big problems for the residents of the building.

4 ▸ Placing underground water tanks in the South-west is a major taboo in Vaastu. It can cause major delays in the life of the building's occupants. These delays could relate to anything, from personal matters to business decisions — anything that has to be finalized or be completed may get delayed.

5 ▸ A basement in the South-west is a huge Vaastu defect as well, and

can make the residents of the house feel depressed and anxious. It can also cause major delays in their life.

6 ▸ The South-west section of the building should be more elevated than the rest of the structure. It should also be heavier in comparison to the North-east.

7 ▸ A kitchen in the South-west corner of the house burns the positive energies that need to be accumulated in this corner. This may result in problems related to reputation and fame for the residents of the house.

8 ▸ Make sure that the South-western wall or corner of your house does not have any cracks, as this could cause health problems, and a consequent increase in expenditure towards the treatment of the same.

Note: The significance and impact of these directions on specific parts and features, such as bedrooms, kitchen, drawing and dining rooms, bathrooms, levels, slopes, etc, of a house or building have been discussed in greater detail in the relevant chapters of each of these topics.

THE FIVE ELEMENTS & SUBTLE ENERGIES

The human body is made up of Panch Mahabhoot Tatvas *or Five Elements — Fire, Water, Air, Space and Earth. It is essential that these elements exist in harmony, both within and outside the body, so that we have a healthy body, a healthy mind as well as a peaceful environment.*

Each element is attributed with some "powers": the element of Space gives the power of sound, the element of Air gives the power of touch, the element of Earth gives shape and structure to the human body, the element of Water provides the required fluids, and the element of Fire creates hunger and heat in the body. Energy, which is important in Vaastu, is officially defined as "the capacity for doing work", and in this sense it is a purely abstract quantity, albeit a very useful one. Electricity, magnetism, light, heat, and motion can all be harnessed to do some work and are all, therefore, forms of energy, and can be measured.

THE ELEMENT OF EARTH

The Earth has a magnetic field and a gravitational force, and these affect everything — whether it is animate or inanimate — on Earth. The Earth is tilted by about 23½ degrees at the meridian. It revolves around the Sun which causes each hemisphere to alternately move closer to and apart from the Sun, thereby causing seasons in a year and a single orbit around the Sun takes 365¼ days (which is called one year). The Earth also rotates on its own axis from the West to the East, which causes day and night.

Three-fourths of the Earth's surface is water and one-fourth is land. The Earth element gives us gravitational energy, and its physical attributes creates shapes, bodies and structure. The Earth element can be land, structure, etc.

It can also influence construction material and the way they are used, and this element provides stability in a structure. One-fourth of your plot has a stronghold on the Earth element. This part is half of the South and West directions. The southern and western corners are essential to harness the Earth element; Vaastu defects will be created if these areas lack the Earth element — say, if basements have been constructed in these areas.

Digging a well or an underground water tank in the South-west of your plot could also cause Vaastu defects. If the building structure is made in the northern and eastern parts of the plot, then the southern and western directions remain vacant and therefore lacks the Earth element. One should not give water slopes towards the South-west; heavy structure or elevation towards the South-west is prosperous.

THE ELEMENT OF SPACE

Space is also called *Ananth*. The solar system and the entire galaxy is "held" by Space. Its effective forces are light, heat, gravitational force and waves, magnetic field and others. Its main property is sound — through the Space element, we get the power of sound.

Space claims the centre of the plot or the "Brahmasthala" which is important in Vaastu science as it is responsible for both growth and expansion. Open areas in the centre create a synergy of the Space element with all the other four elements.

THE ELEMENT OF AIR

Extremely potent, Air is a life-giving element. Pure oxygen is necessary for both brain and blood. Earth's atmosphere contains 21 per cent oxygen (*Praan Vaayu*), 78 per cent nitrogen, and certain proportions of carbon-dioxide, helium, other gases, dust particles, humidity and vapour. Life of human beings, plants, animals and even fire depends on Air.

Where structures are concerned, Vaastu dictates that airflow (in the structure) should zigzag, and the front and rear doors should not face each other. Air should circulate throughout the structure — not come in and flow out immediately. It should be guided to reach each and every corner. Further, do not keep too many decoratives, as they create congestion and hamper the flow of energies in the structure.

The actual corner for Air is the North-west, the presiding deity of which is Vayu, Lord of Air/Wind. In a business organization, the company head and other important employees should not occupy this corner — its fluidity is likely to give rise to confusion and instability: the element of Air means movement.

In a home, the North-west corner should be occupied by girls of marriageable age; it helps expedite marriage. Moreover, the North-western corner should not be overloaded or blocked.

THE ELEMENT OF FIRE

Fire represents light and heat of fire (burning), lightning, volcanic or plutonic heat, the heat of fever or inflammation, energy, days and nights, seasons and such other aspects of the solar system, as well as enthusiasm, ardour, passion, and spirited vigour.

Fire symbolizes life. Under its effect, materials get totally transformed. Raw vegetables and grains get transformed and cooked into food. A hard metal like iron loses shape and takes the form of wires, spirals, and sheets. Gold cannot be polished without Fire. In the human body, Fire creates heat, hunger and thrust.

The mind works best when the element of Fire is moderate; this means that the temperature of the room should be normal — too much heat or too much cold adversely affects the mind and hampers our efficiency.

The South-east direction is owned by Agni, Lord of Fire, and in a building/house, the South-eastern area should be used for fire-related activities. When the Sun reaches the South-east, it releases maximum heat energy in the form of infrared rays. If the South-east is wrongly used, it can — and will — create problems. If you situate your bedroom in the South-east, you and your spouse will probably be irritated with each other and restless most of the times. After all, how can one remain cool in a fireplace?

Moreover, never make a bore well/dig for a water tank or a pipeline or a swimming pool in the South-east — it's quite logical. Fire and Water are anti-elements and juxtaposing them only creates problems like unforeseen issues, unnecessary tensions, litigations, defamation or breakdown of machinery and electronics.

For the same reason, be careful about the placement of Water and Fire elements in your kitchen. Fire can be a truly unmatched friend, but only if you use it well and smartly. It is said that Lord Agnidev, in the form of Fire is always present on our tongues; whatever we speak is burned up. If we talk about our good deeds, Fire "burns" them — in the sense that we lose out on the credit of having helped someone. Conversely, if we confess our bad deeds, we apologize and repent, and those bad deeds get burnt too. So you should never boast about how you helped someone; always confess your bad deeds as these will be negated.

THE ELEMENT OF WATER

Jal or Water is a fundamental element to help in the growth of habitat in this world. This is represented by rain, river, and sea and is in the form of liquid, solid (ice), and gas (steam, cloud). It is a combination of hydrogen and

oxygen in the ratio of 2:1, perfectly neutral in reaction. In every plant and life, Water supports all juices, fluids and blood in our body system. Most of our body functions are based on Water. Likewise, where Vaastu is concerned, if there is sufficient water in a residential structure, it implies a good inflow of funds. In earlier days, rain was related to money.

The presiding deity of Water is Lord Varundev. Keeping a *kalash* full of *gangajal* in the North-east of your residence is very auspicious. It is believed that Lord Vishnu, the Preserver in the Hindu Trinity resides in the *kalash*. So all bore wells and underground water tanks should be positioned in the North-east or North. Underground water tanks and bore wells in the South and South-west create Vaastu defects. No availability of water sources in the North-east can be complemented by creating an artificial water body like a fountain.

Facing the North while drinking water creates abundant wealth. So situate most Water features on the North wall/side of your structure. Mirrors are also identities of Water: placing them on the North wall invites prosperity.

Water bodies are identities which should not be located in bedrooms. This creates instability in relationships. Also check leakage of water from taps — it is symbolic that your money is being wasted or stolen.

SUBTLE ENERGIES

Subtle energies are higher levels of radiation whose detection is beyond the range of most standard physics instrumentation. Subtle energies are the blueprint for the denser forms of electromagnetic energy and matter that make up our physical world. It might be said that everything in the physical world exists first in a subtle energy form.

The universe is full of subtle energies like North Pole energy, electromagnetic energy, Earth's gravitational energy, and solar energy. These energies are very fine; they cannot be seen and can only be sensed.

This vital energy is everywhere; an ever-present force that circulates and moves in the environment. Subtle energy generally flows within the channels and *chakras*. These energies can be sensed, and *chakras* and energy channels are used to receive information in the environment.

These *chakras* are responsible for distributing energy throughout the subtle body. When the body is balanced, these subtle or delicate energies flow freely through the *chakras* and channels, and the physical body is strong and healthy. When there are energy blockages, physical, mental and emotional diseases crop up.

In the same way, if these energies are not permitted to flow properly in the building structure, ie, if it is obstructed by any Vaastu defect like a wrongly-made or incorrectly-placed bathroom, kitchen, or any beam or pillar, the structure is not benefited by the energies, and hence the inmates of the house/building face problems.

When the building is constructed, care should be taken to ensure obstacle-free flow of all the energies mentioned above. These energies can be called life-force energies. If the Vaastu environment is not created according to a harmonious flow and balanced generation of these energies, the inmates of the house will face life problems as the imbalance creates negative energies.

SYMBOLS OF VAASTU

How do symbols affect our lives? Vaastu Shastra uses symbols to create a positive force or energy in our homes and workplaces.

A part of our daily life, a variety of symbols that are used in Vaastu are often used to "decorate" our houses as art objects, or sometimes as sacred objects as well. These symbols, more often than not, signify Hindu concepts and attributes of some Hindu deities, or that of the cosmic truth. Vaastu Shastra uses symbols to create a positive energy in our homes, and to reinforce positive thoughts.

GANESHA

Ganesha can be understood in the form of a symbol as well. His vehicle is a rat, an uncontrollable and problematic creature, which Ganesha brought under his control by making it his vehicle or *vahana.* Ganesha has the power to direct. The noose in his hand is used to trap the unreal, the illusory. Another hand is in the *vara mudra* (giving posture), with which he grants prosperity to the devotee. The *abhaya mudra* (fearless posture) of the fourth hand represents the removal of fear. Ganapati has poverty on his back. On his right should be Goddess Lakshmi, to render prosperity and stability in your home. He likes *modak (laddoo)* as prasad. Tulsi leaves should never be offered to Ganesha.

SWASTIKA

A Swastika represents peaceful energy. Our scriptures tell us that by using and applying the Swastika in our lives, we can bring in prosperity from all directions. It balances all nine directions. The Swastika is used on the main entrance of houses in Gujarat and South India. In the Swastika, the vertical line shows the creation of the universe while the horizontal line shows the expansion. The symbol is also known as the identity of Ganesha. When it is used to remember Ganesha, two vertical lines are drawn on either side to depict his two wives, Riddhi and Siddhi. This combination should be drawn on the main door of the house. In commercial establishments, the words "Shubh" and "Laabh" should also be added on either side of the icon.

AUM

Aum has over a hundred meanings. It invites prosperity, it boosts stability. A reflection of this symbol kills anger, jealousy, fear and ego. Aum is the symbol for existence, and is the sound of the Almighty, from whom all other sounds emerge. Where we cannot place an idol of our God, we should display the symbol of Aum.

KALASH (PITCHER) AND NARIYAL (COCONUT)

All three deities — Brahma, Vishnu, Maheshwar — live in the coconut. If we give a coconut filled with gifts to our near and dear ones, the gifts become auspicious. A coconut placed on the pitcher and kept in the *mandir* is considered very auspicious too. This means the house is full of prosperity and Varundev, Lord of Water, resides there. This symbol should be used on the main door and in the kitchen and *mandir.*

CHARAN (FOOTPRINTS)

Goddess Lakshmi's footprints are made on floors in the form of *rangolis,* usually around main doors, kitchens, *mandirs* and cash lockers, to symbolize her entrance.

VAASTU

at home and in the workplace

PLOTS

The importance of a good plot can be compared to the value attached to a piece of cloth that we purchase for ourself. In both instances, we check the quality, permanence, beauty and other features. The plot for a house or any other structure forms the most basic part of Vaastu, as a positive and auspicious plot can ensure overall prosperity.

The necessity of inspecting a plot before purchasing it cannot be and should not be underestimated. This point holds immense significance, because once you purchase unsuitable land, as per Vaastu standards, and build a house there, it is extremely difficult, and in most cases impossible, to rectify it.

There are certain procedures that one can follow to test the goodness or virtue of a plot of land.

1. The best way, according to me, is to go to the plot and take ten deep breaths. Close your eyes while doing this and try to feel the vibrations of the land. If you feel relaxed or happy, the property is probably good. If you think you are not attuned enough to sense the vibrations, you can take a more intuitive or sensitive person to the land or even take a newborn child to the plot. If the child remains happy and laughs, the plot is good.

2. Another method involves digging a 1.5ft-deep pit in the centre of the plot. Fill this pit with water and wait for a few minutes. If the water level in the pit goes down by 60 per cent, you should not purchase the plot; if the water level goes down by less than 50 per cent, the plot is average; and if the level of water remains the same

or goes down only by around 10 per cent, the plot is very good and powerful, and definitely worth purchasing.

3 ▸ Check the land by taking the soil in one hand and holding it tightly. After a few minutes, slowly open your hand. If the soil slips out quickly from your hand, the land is not good. However, if the soil sticks to your hand and doesn't slide out easily, the land can be termed as good.

FACTORS TO CHECK OUT BEFORE BUYING A PLOT

1 ▸ Make sure that your building is not located next to or near a graveyard or hospital. Both these places emit a lot of negative energies in the area, and in the case of the latter, probably many infections as well!

2 ▸ It is not advisable to build a structure near a temple or a church, as the apexes of both these houses of worship release the negative energies of the followers. However, if your house is near a temple or church, try to ensure that its shadow does not fall on your building.

3 ▸ The presence of a big industrial building near or in front of your

building causes problems in growth and development for you and other occupants of your house. You should also make sure that your land is not squashed between two large buildings.

4 ▸ A river to the South of your building is not considered Vaastu-friendly. Similarly, there should not be any mountains or large buildings to the North of your house.

5 ▸ Properties that are covered with green vegetation, trees, plants and grass are good. Agriculturally fertile land is also known as live land. Corner plots are very auspicious.

6 ▸ The main entry of the plot should not have an electric pole, telephone pole or a big tree in front of it. A plot that faces a road ending or a T-junction is also not good.

7 ▸ Make sure that the plot does not contain garbage or stones.

8 ▸ Plots that are surrounded by running roads from all directions are considered good for commercial purposes.

9 ▸ Plots that face the North are considered the most auspicious, followed by the East, West, and lastly, the South.

10 ▸ If the North-east corner of a plot has a natural slope and its South-west corner is high, it is very prosperous.

PLOTS ACCORDING TO VARNA (CATEGORY)

According to Vaastu scriptures, square-shaped plots, with white-coloured soil, an udambra tree, and a slope towards the North are the most suitable and fortunate for Brahmins. Moreover, the soil of this plot should be sweet to taste.

In the case of Kshatriyas, the shape of the plot should be rectangular; its length should be one-eighth more than its width. The soil's colour should ideally be of a reddish shade, and its flavour a little bitter. The slope of the land should be towards the East. This type of site guarantees success to Kshatriyas.

For Vaishyas, the length of the plot should be one-sixth more than its width; the soil's colour should have yellowish shades, and it should taste sour. The slope of the land should head towards the East.

Plots whose length is one-fourth more than its width, and where the soil's colour is blackish and has a pungent flavour are best suited for Shudras. These sites make them feel good and invites prosperity.

In general, all the sites mentioned above should be free of ants, worms, potsherds, pebbles and bones. They should also be free from holes and cavities, and be as smooth as a sheet.

SHAPES AND SIZES OF PLOTS

Square plots

Plots whose length equals their breadth are called square plots. These types of plots are believed to be very lucky and prosperous, and invite happiness in one's life. The Vaastu Purush fits very easily within square plots. However, since plots of this shape are very rarely available, one can instead make their rooms in this proportion.

Rectangular plots

The length of these plots is bigger than their width, and their corners have 90-degree angles. These types of plots are very prosperous; their Vaastu layout can be designed easily. One should take care that the length and width should be within the ratio of 2:1, ie, the length should not be more than the double of the width. If the length is more than double the width, the occupants of that plot do not get a regular flow of energy. Such plots also create disagreements within the family. In some cases, a rectangular plot is created by divisions in the family, where the plot is cut and divided along its length.

Triangular plots

These are three-sided plots, with 45-degree angle corners. Although triangular plots are very rare, one should not purchase them even if they are available. Plots of this shape can cause a great many problems in all aspects of one's life, and residents of such plots are always in trouble.

Corner-cut plots

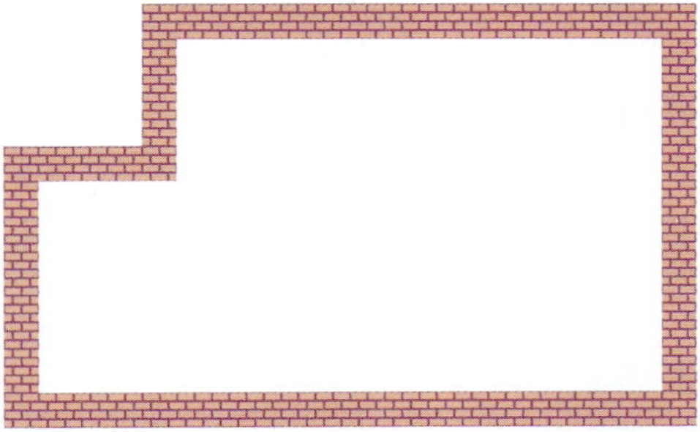

Areas where one corner of the plot is not parallel to the other corners or the sides of a plot are not of a regular shape are not considered good. Building a structure on such a plot is not at all auspicious, as these types of plots cause restlessness, financial crunches and a flood of diseases. Vaastu defects in these plots, however, can be rectified by diverting the flow of subtle energies.

Circular plots

These plots are very rare but extremely good for attracting wealth and prosperity. Circular plots bring overall growth in the lives of its occupants.

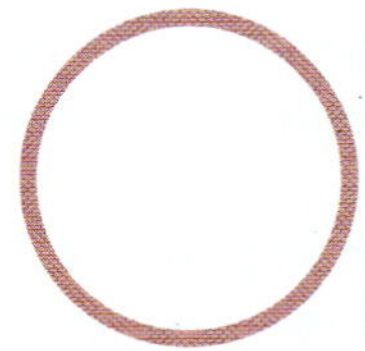

Oval plots

These kinds of plots are very inauspicious, and lead to big losses in life.

Semicircular plots

A D-shaped plot is considered very inauspicious and, like oval plots, bring financial problems in life.

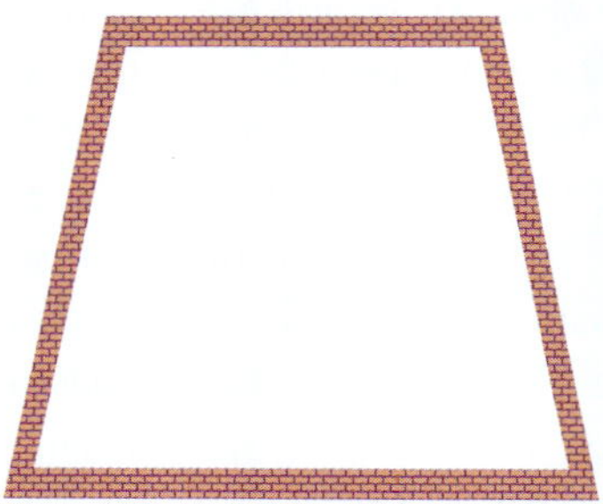

Gomukh plots

In these types of plots, the width of their front side is less than that of the back. These plots are good for residential use, and should not be used for commercial purposes. However, one must take care that a gomukh plot does not face the North, as this results in a shortening of this auspicious direction. Such plots are even then not good for residential purposes.

Singhmukh plots

In these kinds of plots, the width of their front side is more than that of the back. These plots are not good for residential purposes, but are acceptable as commercial establishments.

VAASTU FOR NEW STRUCTURES

Now that you have bought the plot of your choice, remember, on this extremely happy and momentous day of your life, that Vaastu Shastra offers some suggestions that will, if followed well, make your future a pleasant and harmonious one. Whether you will be constructing a house or an office building, use Vaastu to make it work to your advantage.

When and where to start construction, ideal directions and days, Vaastu defects to avoid, elements to incorporate and things to keep in mind... here's a comprehensive dos/don'ts list, simple to remember, easy to follow. And while you are about it, do check out a few things outside your building/house.

THINGS TO DO BEFORE YOU START CONSTRUCTION

Bhoomi Pujan

Before starting construction of any new structure, one should worship one's *kuldevta*, Lord Ganesha, Lord Kshetrapal, the Vaastu Purush and the Dikpatis (lords of the directions). Make sure that you give the construction labourers good rewards when you start the building process.

Auspicious days and directions

Monday, Wednesday, Thursday, Friday and Saturday are auspicious days to start construction. Digging should be started from the North-eastern direction and the structure should be built from southern to western directions. The construction should not end in the South.

Hot Tip: Use square and solid bricks for laying the foundation.

Alter with caution

While building our house or any other structure, if we find that it is not properly planned we always make some changes. For example, if any part of the construction is not made according to our requirement, we break it and try to change it. Please note that the main door of the house or structure should not be altered while construction is going on.

MORE THINGS TO REMEMBER

Always leave some open space on all four sides of the structure, as well as earthen, non-concrete space. Ensure that sunlight reaches each and every room of the structure. A common wall shared by adjacent plot owners is not good Vaastu. Sharing walls means sharing luck, so avoid it. Try making a new, individual boundary wall for yourself.

Keep the structure to a regular shape — rectangular or square. The corners of the building should not be cut.

Do not use old bricks, old iron parts or old wood to make a new house. All these things store past energies. Avoid positioning water sources in the South, even for construction purposes.

VAASTU FOR BUILDINGS

Once you have Vaastu-proofed your building structure, it's time to add these final touches for health, wealth and felicity.

Tilak

Wearing a *tilak* invokes a sense of purity and stability. It covers the *Ajna Chakra*, the area between your eyebrows which is the reservoir for intuition, memory and better thought. Applying a *tilak* frees you from worries, helps you take decisions and helps you to keep your cool. In ancient times, people were classified into the four *varnas* of Brahmin, Kshatriya, Vaishya, Shudra. The *tilak* application would vary according to one's *varna*. Brahmins applied white sandal (signifying purity and peace) with the index finger. Kshatriyas applied red *kumkum* (symbolizing strength and stability) with the thumb and in an upward direction. Vaishyas applied saffron or turmeric (denoting wealth and prosperity) with the middle finger. Shudras applied black *bhasma* or *vibhuti* (representing dedication).

You can apply a *tilak* on your building too! Apply the *tilak* at the centre of the building, about 6–8ft from the ground, as well as on every door, except the bathroom door; this is very auspicious. Now, the type and colour of the *tilak* will depend on what it is that you seek to achieve:

White sandal: For peace and calmness.

Red *kumkum*: To counter depression, lethargy, lack of ambition, vigour.

Yellow saffron or turmeric: To attract wealth and financial prosperity.

Black *bhasma*: To impose control, also to eliminate negativity.

AUSPICIOUS SYMBOLS

Display pious and beautiful symbols like the Swastika, *Kalash*, Aum and the

feet of Goddess Lakshmi to counterbalance negativity and enhance prosperity. Apply a Swastika or Aum-shaped *tilak* to your building to gain power and prosperity. You can also apply a u-shaped *tilak* to symbolize Lord Vishnu's feet to bring in prosperity.

Some people hang demonic face masks outside their houses to ward off negative energies, but this is inauspicious. Moreover, do remember not to put pictures of deities outside; you can't possibly benefit by leaving your gods outside in harsh sunlight, rain and storm while you sit in comfort inside!

NAILS

Avoid hammering lead or steel nails on walls to suspend decoratives or other items. Use brass screws instead.

FRONT COURTYARD

Ensure that the front courtyard of your building isn't damaged or worn out, as this might result in tensions in your family.

FRONT WALL

A dilapidated front wall increases your vulnerability to litigations. Make sure that all the walls are intact and well-maintained.

THE EXTERIOR TOO IS IMPORTANT

In addition to the rules laid down by Vaastu Shastra for houses/buildings, there are things that need to be checked outside the structure as well.

PLANTS AND TREES

Ashoka

Planting this in the South and West blocks out negative energies. A *toran* of Ashoka leaves at the main door invites prosperity.

Tulsi

Along with religious and cultural values, it also has medicinal value. Tending to a tulsi plant counters many Vaastu defects. Keep it in the North-east or centre of the house.

Pomegranate

Planting this in the plot's East is very auspicious.

Jamun

Plant this in the South and West but never plant a barren one.

Banana

This should be planted in the North, and worshipped if within the plot's boundaries.

Mango

Do not plant a mango tree in your house, but never cut an existing one either.
Remember: Keekar and tamarind trees within the boundaries of your plot are not auspicious.

LANDSCAPING

North

Rockeries or elevated stone arrangements in the plot's North stop money inflow, cause business losses and hinder promotion and growth. Burdening the North home of Lord Kuber also means blocking opportunities for creating wealth.

North-east

Such landscaping in the North-east creates health problems and invites unnecessary tension for the plot occupants. The North-eastern, owned by Lord Shiva encourages the flow of electromagnetic energy and should be allowed to flow free. Positioning heavy rocks there can hamper both the name and fame of occupants.

WATER

Pools, water reservoirs, borings

When situated in the plot's South, these can cause unforeseen problems, litigation issues, accidents and major surgeries. This also applies to the South-east, which is the repository of the Fire element — the anti-element of Water.

Flows and slopes

All rainwater and drainage slopes should be constructed in the northern side of the plot. This invites prosperity and wealth-creation opportunities for the family.

MAIN DOOR & ENTRIES

The main door of any building plays an extremely important role in Vaastu, and accounts for at least 15–20 per cent of this ancient science. This is because it allows the entry of good or bad luck into the building all the time. Hence, it is imperative to take great care while deciding on the location of the main entry.

The main door of a dwelling is given utmost importance in Vaastu Shastra because it reflects the first impression, beauty, personality and the well-being of the occupants. Furthermore, the front door is regarded as the "face" of the house and this is why emphasis is given to its location and the direction it faces. As the "face" of a house and the main inlet of positive energies, it is critical to get the entrance right.

As you begin constructing your home, do remember that direction plays an important role in the location of the main door of the house.

NORTH

Placing the main entry in this direction is very auspicious. The main gate or door should be located in the third, fourth and fifth part of the North direction. Make sure that you are able to see the gate while standing inside the building and looking out.

EAST

This direction represents prosperity. A main gate/door in the East should be positioned in the third and fourth part of this direction.

WEST

A main gate/door in the West should be placed in the fourth and fifth part of this direction. The West is not very auspicious. According to some scriptures, Lord Varundev represents the West.

SOUTH

Looked upon as an unlucky direction, the South can prove to be quite prosperous if the main entry is positioned well. A main gate/door in the South should be placed in the third and fourth part of the direction.

Note: All entry parts are counted from left to right, while facing the specific direction.

MAIN DOOR

This chief access point is the face of a house and should be taken care of in the same way as we take care of our face each morning. There are two aspects to ensuring the creation of an auspicious main door — one is the direction in which it is located and the other is its general maintenance and upkeep.

1. As mentioned above and in the chapter on Directions, you can see that placing the main door in any of the eight directions, according to their usage, has its own share of positive and negative effects. However, I would like to add that the South-west is probably the worst direction for placing the main door. This causes problems

and delays in various spheres of your life. This is because the magnetic energy emanating from the North-east should ideally get accumulated in the South-west, but a door in this corner results in it all leaking out.

2 ▸ The main door should not only be bigger than all the other doors in the house, its dimensions should also be as defined by Vaastu. Ideally, its length and breadth ratio should be 1:2. In some buildings, due to the low height of the ceiling, the height of the door is low; while in others, due to shortage of space, the width of the door is less. This creates problems in energy flows related to opportunities and wealth.

3 ▸ The main door should also be the most attractive door in the building. It is believed that Goddess Lakshmi enters houses whose doors are beautifully maintained. The same stands true of positive energy as well. Hence, it is important that the main door is kept clean at all times, and is not worn out.

4 ▸ The door should be decorated by auspicious symbols such as an image of the *kalash*, with coconut on it, Goddess Lakshmi's *charan* (feet) pointing towards the house, or a Swastika with "Riddhi Siddhi" and "Shubh Laabh" written on either side of the symbol —

the Swastika represents Lord Ganesha, while Riddhi and Siddhi are his two wives, and Shubh and Laabh are his two sons.

5 A *toran* or *bhandanwar* is a good ornament for the main door. It invites good luck and wards off bad energies.

6 Placing a lit *diya* (earthenware oil lamp) outside the main door at sunset is a good custom. It helps ward off any negative energies, and also works as a security measure against evil forces.

7 Creaking sounds made by un-oiled doors kill the positive energy that is about to enter or already exists in the building. Make sure that you lubricate the hinges of all doors (main doors, room doors, cupboard doors, etc.) at regular intervals to put an end to these sounds. This applies to creaking windows as well.

8 The main door should open inward into the house, and towards the left. This allows energy to enter and flow freely. Doors that open towards the right or outwards are not considered auspicious.

9 Make sure that there is no door, within the building or outside, which faces the main door when you open it.

10 ▸ The presence of a small opening above the main door, in the form of a ventilator, is very auspicious.

11 ▸ You also need to check the presence of any *vedh shools* (sharp arrows of energy) outside your building. These *vedh shools* can take many forms. For instance, buildings ending or situated at the T-end of a road are not auspicious; a big tree, pole, big wall or building in front of the main door is not good either. Placing bright lights in front of your building is one of the remedies to correct the defects created by the *shool*.

UNWANTED FEATURES IN FRONT OF YOUR MAIN DOOR

Door

It causes problems related to health, family and conception.

Tree

It may intensify behavioral problems in children, hamper prosperity and affect your health.

Flowing water feature

You may suffer unnecessary expenses.

Well

Causes body aches and stomach problems, creates fears.

Temple

There will be problems aplenty for the head of the family. Additionally, children will suffer from overall stagnation.

Temple's door

It can cause severe financial problems.

Big pole/pillar

It leads to health problems for women and the untimely death of the head of the family.

Garbage heap

It makes the lady of the house depressed and confused.

Major wall

It impoverishes the entire family.

Graveyard (even within 200m)

It may invite bad spirits and evil.

Door to another house

It leads to financial losses and problems.

Edge of another house

Leads to accidents and losses in every aspect.

॥ श्री ॥
शुभ लाभ
ॐ
शुभ लाभ

MANDIR

The mandir *or prayer room holds a very special position in a house. It is a place of devotion, hope, trust, truth, and even refuge. In view of the* mandir's *immense significance, it is essential to create a space that embodies the best possible principles of Vaastu.*

The best direction to worship in is the North-east. In Vaastu science, the North-east corner is known as *isshan* (corner for *ishwar* or God). This direction is recognized as the point from where Earth's powerful magnetic energy is generated. Therefore, this is an ideal location for a *mandir*. However, if your *mandir* is not situated in the North-east, make sure that you face this direction while praying.

1 ▸ Wood and marble are the best materials to use when constructing a *mandir*.

2 ▸ Make sure that the *mandir* is not positioned next to the bathroom. One should also avoid building a *mandir* in the bedroom or the kitchen.

3 ▸ Don't build a *mandir* underneath the stairs, or construct any structure over it, as you would end up symbolically stepping on it.

4 ▸ The idols and images should be placed on a wooden platform. Rose wood is a good wood to use here. Do not use ply or laminated wood. The idols can be placed on marble and stone as well.

5 Make sure that the size of the idols is not more than the size of the thumb of the owner of the house. This is because idols that are bigger than the thumb are usually placed in a community *mandir*. These idols undergo a *pran prathishta* ceremony, whereby they are symbolically filled with power. After this ritual, the idol is taken care of as a human being, because it is believed that the idol now has *prana* energy (life energy) in it.

6 Avoid placing too many pictures or symbols of a single God.

7 Make it a point to light a *diya* or burn incense before the gods in your *mandir* every evening.

8 Never place pictures of deceased people or your guru in the *mandir*. This is because the deceased and gurus are human beings, and as such, have a lower position in comparison to God.

9 Placing pictures, idols and tiles of Lord Ganesha on gates and at the front of a house is not advisable. Goddess Lakshmi's sister Daridrata, whose name means poverty, is featured on Lord Ganesha's back. So, when you place the God with His back to the house, you are, in essence, inviting poverty into your house.

DRAWING ROOM

The drawing room has long been considered as both a place of prestige and a showcase of one's personality and individuality. Most of the time, all formal and distinguished guests are invited first to this room, and it usually gives the first impression of the house and its residents. As such, people make it a point to transform their drawing room into the most beautiful area of the house.

The drawing room, the room where you entertain your guests, may well be regarded as the "public" area in your home, as anybody and everybody cannot be permitted to enter the further interiors of your house. It serves the purpose of meeting people to either entertain or for other need-based discussions.

Guests should feel welcome and at ease here, and this can happen only if positive energies flow here. So, in addition to beautifying your drawing room, create a harmonious Vaastu environment to make it an auspicious room as well.

1. The best possible location for a drawing room is in the East, North or North-west directions.

2. The North-east portion of the drawing room should be kept spacious and as free of furniture as possible. The East side should also be kept light and airy.

3. All heavy furniture should be placed next to the walls on the southern and western sides of the drawing room.

4. The seating arrangement should be such that while sitting, one faces the East direction.

5. Placing a mirror on the northern wall helps enhance the positive effects of the energies emanating from the North. The northern wall is also a good place for installing windows, as this brings in prosperity. If the northern and eastern walls are enhanced, the inmates of that structure become prosperous.

6. While decorating your drawing room, make it a point to showcase your most priceless possessions here. The theory behind this is that the wealth you display will multiply and come back to you manifold. It is said that whatever you display and see, is what you will receive: so display your wealth, good art pieces, your achievements, etc, in the drawing hall.

7. Make sure that the drawing room is well lit. Also, pastel green is an auspicious colour for the walls. It is important to leave the northern and eastern walls for light-weighed furniture. Heavy furniture should not be kept against northern and eastern walls.

8. Beautifying your drawing room with fresh flowers and plants is very auspicious. Yellow and red flowers especially help create a dynamic

and prosperous environment. Avoid using dried or artificial flowers, and make sure that dead flowers are replaced as soon as possible.

9 ▸ Good fragrances are both healthy and necessary to maintain a good environment. Aroma oils can be used to enhance the environments. Aromatic fragrances such as incense and essential oils of flowers are pious and have cleansing properties, and are highly conducive to creating a positive environment as they attract angels and deities. Light and burn them regularly to clear the house of negative energy forms. A fragrant environment is liked by angels and gods. Keeping a bowl full of sea salt in the house helps to keep the negative energies at bay.

10 ▸ Be sure to place bowls filled with sea salt around the room as this substance has great negativity extracting powers.

11 ▸ Quartz crystals are famous for their amazing cleansing properties, and are a very powerful tool in both cleaning negative energies and enhancing the room and building's positive environment. Be sure to place some around the living room.

12 ▸ The presence of a Water element in the North-east makes the positive energy of this direction even stronger. One can keep a

fountain, with fresh running water, or a bowl of flowers filled with fresh water in this corner for prosperity. Water elements on the North and North-eastern walls give prosperous life to the inmates of the structure.

13 Keeping idols or pictures of various gods and goddesses in the drawing room is not advisable.

14 Do not keep any kind of dead objects in your drawing and dining rooms, or anywhere else in the house. These include dried flowers, broken articles or utensils, wild animal skins or antiques. The last usually contains the energies of the user and may be inauspicious. Keeping stuffed dead animals should also be avoided.

15 Do not hang your wall clocks, timepieces and calendars in the southern, South-eastern and South-western directions — it brings an unfavourable phase in your life. Also check that clocks and calendars should not be placed above the doors. All clocks placed in the house or office should be in working condition; if it is not working, wrap them in paper or box and store them in cupboards.

Led Zeppelin
EAT MY
SHORTS

DINING ROOM

These days, either due to a shortage of space or due to the general architectural layout of the area, the dining room usually presents itself as an extension of the drawing room. The dining room is an area where the members of a family enjoy their meals, and thus it plays an important role in promoting health and harmony among the family members.

Mealtimes, when the entire family gets together for the first and last meals of the day, and enjoys each other's company is very important — more so nowadays when, thanks to the hectic pace of life, family members hardly find time to spend with one another. This is where they should eat a nourishing meal, which will benefit them. Relationships within the family get strengthened when the family sits and eats together.

1. Try to face the East, North, North-east or North-west while having food, as these are very auspicious directions.

2. Always display fresh fruits on the dining table. You can also use fresh flowers to decorate the dining table.

3. Installing a large mirror on the eastern wall of the dining room so that it reflects the fruit and food laid out on the table has a multiplying effect. This brings in prosperity.

4. Sharp utensils such as knives and scissors should be kept covered at all times. Displaying these or leaving them out in the open can give rise to bad or unpleasant relationships with family and friends.

Similarly, pickles should also be kept in a covered place as an open display can create sourness in relationships.

5 Avoid using an oval-shaped dining table, as it is inauspicious.

6 The dining table should not be visible from the main door. A curtain or a false partition can be used as a screen.

7 Make sure that the furniture in the dining room does not overshadow the dining table, which should stand out. This enhances the family's prosperity.

8 Focusing light from the ceiling on to the dining table also helps increase prosperity.

9 Avoid placing the dining table along a wall; it should have enough space on all sides.

10 The dining table should have an even number of chairs, ie, two, four, six and so on. This is believed to be very auspicious.

11 Displaying medicines is again a strict no-no; remember: what you see is what you get.

KITCHEN

Everyone can understand the significance of a kitchen. After all, a house without a kitchen cannot be considered complete. An Indian housewife spends most of her time in the kitchen — her day starts in the kitchen and ends in the kitchen — and the entire family gets their basic life energy from food that is prepared in the kitchen. One can even say that the kitchen is the backbone of the house.

In earlier times, the kitchen was situated in an open space. This helped the kitchen access as much light as possible and made it easier to dispel smoke rising from the stove. Today, most of us have closed kitchens. Hence, it is essential to create a Vaastu-friendly kitchen that fulfils the requirement for a place that takes care of our physical, emotional and biological needs.

1. The kitchen should, ideally, be located between the southern and eastern directions, ie, in the South-east direction of the plot. Kitchens situated in the North-eastern direction may result in heavy losses for the family. Similarly, kitchens in the South-west could give rise to clashes within the family, whereas a kitchen in the North-west may result in an increase in expenditure.

2. Good lighting is an essential prerequisite for a kitchen. To ensure proper ventilation and a positive Vaastu environment, the kitchen's windows should be positioned in the eastern direction. Artificial lighting should also be sufficient.

3. The best place for the kitchen door is in the North. Take care that while preparing food, the cook does not have his/her back towards a door.

4 ▸ The kitchen is an important place in the house. It should be painted with fiery colours like red, orange, yellow, brown, etc; blue and black shades are a strict no-no. Avoid using blue as it is identified with Water. Shades of green can be used as a remedy for improving the Vaastu of wrongly-placed kitchens.

5 ▸ Avoid placing the cooking stove on the North-eastern corner. It should be on the eastern wall of the kitchen or in the South-east corner of the kitchen area. This direction is called *Agneya Disha*, named after Agni, the Hindu god of fire who resides here. This *disha* (direction) has a natural source of Fire as solar heat is at its maximum when the sun is in the southern direction. When the sun reaches the South-east, it releases vitamins D and F in the atmosphere. The value of these vitamins in the kitchen is immeasurable.

6 ▸ All heat-generating kitchen equipment, such as microwaves, hot cases, hotplates, geysers, mixer grinders, etc, should also be placed in the South-east direction of the kitchen.

7 ▸ While preparing the food, the cook should face the East or the South. Facing the North or the West while cooking is not favourable. The cook or the housewife, whoever is cooking, should

not have his/her back towards the kitchen door while cooking.

8 ▸ Since the element of Water is the opposite of Fire, great care should be taken about its positioning. All Water arrangements should be placed in the North or the North-east, as this is considered very auspicious. Also ensure that all Water elements are situated to the left of the gas stove. The placement should be such that when you use the gas stove for cooking, water utilities such as washbasins, sinks, and drinking water are on your left.

9 ▸ Avoid placing a refrigerator in the kitchen, as the elements of Water and Fire clash with each other.

10 ▸ Store all heavy grains and raw foods in the South and West directions of the kitchen. This is because, as per the principles of Vaastu, these directions should be occupied with heavy objects. The southern and western walls should be made heavy by keeping heavy groceries and utensils. Closets and kitchen cupboards can be put up here.

11 ▸ The kitchen's northern and eastern corners should be kept free of clutter and not blocked with heavy materials or equipments.

12 ▸ The *mandir* should not be made in the kitchens. Try not to keep pictures of gods and goddesses in the kitchen.

13 ▸ Cleanliness and hygiene is also a must.

**See Appendix for case studies of kitchens.*

BEDROOM

The bedroom represents a sanctuary, a place to take refuge from the stressful outside world. In fact, on an average, a person spends almost one-third of his/her life in the bedroom. Therefore, keeping the considerable importance of this room in mind, it is essential that its location, the placement of furniture within it and other relevant factors are arranged in a manner that is conducive to creating a positive and favourable Vaastu environment.

A place to unwind, relax and restore oneself... that's the importance of the bedroom for you! The direction in which you sleep affects your work ability and private life. If your bedroom is not in the correct direction, then you can suffer from disturbed sleep, restlessness, health problems and frequent fights with your spouse. In short, you can be totally bereft of any peace in your life.

1 ▸ The South-west direction of the plot is, undoubtedly, the best possible location for a bedroom. This is a very restful and powerful area, and the main breadwinner of the house should occupy the bedroom here.

2 ▸ Newly-married couples should not occupy a bedroom located in the South-west area of the house, especially if they live within a joint family. This can lead to friction between the bride and her in-laws. A bedroom in or near the North-west corner would be preferable, if possible.

3 ▸ Pregnant women should not stay in a bedroom that is situated in the North-east corner of the house, as staying in a room in this direction may increase the chances of a miscarriage.

4 ▸ Unmarried girls in the family should be given a bedroom in the North-west section of the house. This direction is not, however, auspicious for couples, and those residing in this corner may suffer from asthma, breathing disorders, coughs and colds.

5 ▸ According to Vaastu, the South-east is the ideal place for fire and other related gadgets. Hence, couples should not position their bedroom in this direction, as it may cause high blood pressure and chronic irritability, resulting in clashes in their marital relations.

6 ▸ The positioning of the bed in the bedroom is very important as well. Make sure that there is a solid wall behind the bed. Never sleep in a bed that has windows behind it. This position of the bed usually leads to instability in the occupant's life. The bed should also not point towards the wall of the bathroom; and a bed that adjoins the bathroom wall receives negative energy from that direction, which could result in health problems for the occupant.

7 ▸ Always remember to point your head towards the South while sleeping. This will help you sleep soundly. People who sleep with their head pointed towards the North usually experience restless and troubled sleep through the night, as they are lying down against the direction of the electromagnetic waves travelling from

the North. This then results in headaches and body aches when they wake up the next morning.

8 ▸ Another important point to take care of is that, when lying down, do not point your feet towards the door of the room, as this is considered inauspicious. It may lead to many health problems.

9 ▸ Couples should make sure that they share the same bed, mattress and sheets. This increases harmony in relationships.

10 ▸ Bed sheets and pillow covers should be replaced every six months as they absorb all the negativity that you shed on them while sleeping.

11 ▸ When decorating your bedroom, choose positive colours like pink, light green, light blue and very light purple for the overall colour scheme. Pure white is a good colour for creating a spiritual atmosphere. Do not choose dull or sharp colours for the bedroom.

12 ▸ Avoid placing heavy furniture in the North-east corner of the bedroom. Also, try to keep this corner free of clutter.

13 ▸ Never hang pictures of animals fighting, hunting lions, fire scenes,

war scenes, trees devoid of flowers and fruits, and dead animals — especially of pigeons, crows, snakes, vultures and owls.

14 ▸ Do not display pictures of gods or goddesses in the bedroom. The reason for this is that the bedroom is a private place, where we sit, sleep, relax, drink and enjoy the various pleasures of life. Indulging in these activities in front of images of gods is considered disrespectful.

15 ▸ Try to avoid placing mirrors in the bedroom. Their presence can lead to unnecessary quarrels between couples. If a mirror is an essential requirement in your bedroom, make sure that it is positioned in a way whereby it does not reflect your image while sleeping.

16 ▸ Be aware of what you place under your bed or around you when you sleep. According to the principle of proximity, objects placed close to you have a stronger effect on you. And, the longer the period of exposure, the more intense is the effect, whether beneficial or harmful. If you use the area under your bed for storage, consider the effect it has had on you, especially if you haven't been sleeping well. Many people keep shoes under the bed. This can keep you "running around" all night, even when you

are sound asleep. Clothes lying under or on the bed carry many life experiences, and do not make for relaxing "sleeping partners". Books or work-related papers stimulate you intellectually. Hence, if you are finding it difficult to switch your mind into rest mode, make sure you are not sleeping on top of a lot of information. Items such as utensils, knives and other junk are not meant to be under your bed, and can cause strained relationships and confusions.

17 Avoid keeping a television in your bedroom as it emits electromagnetic radiation that may be harmful to you.

18 Avoid installing cash lockers in the bedroom. A safe can be kept but only in the South-west corner of the bedroom, and it should open facing the northern or eastern directions.

19 Water is an unstable element and hence has no place in your bedroom. This includes aquariums and water fountains, etc. Objects such as these may cause instability in your life.

20 Placing windows on the East side of a bedroom is very beneficial since this direction receives positive energies from the sun as it rises. The ultraviolet rays of the sun are believed to be very good for health, and also eliminate any negative energy present in the room.

21 ▸ The presence of a beam in your bedroom may cause health problems and tensions in your life. One possible way of avoiding unnecessary stress in life is by not sleeping under the beam.

**See Appendix for case studies of bedrooms.*

BATHROOM

According to Vaastu scriptures, the bathroom is one of the most sensitive zones in a house or building. In earlier times, the bathroom was positioned outside the house, but in today's day and age, it forms a part of the inner sanctum of the modern home. Therefore, it is imperative to maintain perfect hygiene and cleanliness, not only in terms of the physical world but also in terms of Vaastu energies.

The bathroom is that place where we cleanse ourselves and which releases negative energies. Additionally, this is that place which if not kept totally spic and span, will be a breeding ground for germs and bacteria. This makes the location of the bathroom important from the Vaastu point of view. Incorrect placement can create havoc in the lives of the occupants of the house.

1. The best direction for a bathroom is the North-west. This is an Air element direction and, as a result, does not hamper the flow of subtle energies.

2. Placing a bathroom in the North-east corner of a house is a severe Vaastu offence. The North-east is a very pious place, owned by Lord Shiva and occupied by the Vaastu Purush's forehead. The North-east is a point from where electromagnetic energies emanate, and the entire building is imbued by this energy. If a bathroom is placed here, it contaminates these energies. Hence, installing a bathroom here can cause disastrous health issues, accidents, and problems with progeny as well as unnecessary tensions.

3. Positioning a bathroom in the South-east area is also a problem as

per Vaastu principles. This is because this area is occupied by the Fire element and owned by Lord Agnidev, while a bathroom is a part of the Water element, which acts in opposition to Fire. A bathroom here also shows disrespect to Lord Agnidev. The residents of the building with a bathroom in the South-east may have to face unexpected losses, legal issues, taxation problems and electricity-related mishaps or accidents.

4 ▸ Similarly, a bathroom in the South-west is inauspicious as well, and can result in financial losses and unnecessary expenses for the residents of the building. In some cases, they also experience feelings of anxiety and depression. Since the North-east's magnetic energy is stored in this direction, there should ideally be no drainage in this area.

5 ▸ The bathroom should also not be placed in the centre of the house because Lord Brahma resides in this pious location. Moreover, the central area is the point from where gravitational energy emanates, and a bathroom here would infect this positive energy.

6 ▸ The bathroom should not be visible when entering a building.

7 ▸ Make sure that the bathroom is not attached to the kitchen wall or

to the wall of the *mandir.* The bathroom releases a lot of negative energies and is not clean; it may affect the sanctity of the kitchen and the food cooked therein may get contaminated. The same stands true for the *mandir*: the holy environment does not remain pure and clean because of the bathroom's negative energies, other than being disrespectful to the gods.

8 ▸ The commode should be positioned in a way that a person does not face the sun while using it. A person should face the North, North-west or West when using it, as the sun does not travel in these directions.

9 ▸ The shower apparatus and taps should be installed on the northern wall of the bathroom. The North has a Water element, and using water when facing the North attracts financial prosperity.

10 ▸ Bathrooms should be kept pristine and uncluttered, not decorated. Avoid constructing storage space inside the bathroom.

**See Appendix for case studies of bathrooms/washrooms.*

VAASTU FOR CHILDREN'S ROOM & STUDY

Children are not only the future of the nation, but also, in a sense, the epitome of their parents' hopes, dreams and aspirations. And parents want nothing but the very best for their children. In today's stressful life situation, we, as parents, can gift them a pleasant, soothing Vaastu-perfect life, which will ease their tension and subsequent pressure.

As we have already read, Vaastu affects all of us either positively or negatively, and children are not outside this "reach". Their immediate environment can either work adversely or beneficially for them. A Vaastu-wise harmonious surrounding will make them happy and well-balanced, enabling them to carry out their work and play cheerfully and in the correct manner. A few easy dos and don'ts are all that it takes to ensure a positive environment now, which will assuredly give them a better tomorrow.

1 Children's bedroom should never be in the South-western side as they will become more powerful and try to dominate other family members.

2 The best rooms for children are on western or southern sides of the plot, but all corners should definitely be avoided for the children's room.

3 The study room should be in the East, North or the North-east directions of the house: greater absorption of power and increase in knowledge is available in these areas.

4. Students should also try to face the East or North which will help in quicker learning and improve memory as well as concentration.

5. Books should always be kept in the South-west, South or West directions and not in the North-east.

6. Open bookshelves are not good; always try to keep the books in shelves or closed areas with glass panel doors. Open bookshelves create too much congestion in the mind.

7. Again, loads of books on the table create unnecessary pressure on the mind, so books should not be kept on tables as well.

8. The study room should have images of Lord Ganesha and Goddess Saraswati.

9. Mothers should make sure that when children go to bed, their heads should rest in the South direction. It helps in maintaining the magnetic balance of the body with that of the Earth.

10. Vaastu-wise, the study table should not "stick" to the wall. There should be a solid wall behind the child as one sits at the desk. If there is a window at your back, keep the curtains or blinds closed.

11 ▸ When studying, be sure not to sit with your back to the door. The study table and the chair must not face the door.

12 ▸ Good lighting in the study area is very important; it should properly spread in each and every corner. One should avoid spotlights and sharp lights, as this heightens the child's mental pressure and strain.

13 ▸ A quartz crystal rock in the South-west corner helps to further energize the Earth element and enhance the positive energy in the study area. It is a beautiful instrument to extract the negative energies of the environment.

14 ▸ Placing an Amethyst crystal on the study table helps the child to concentrate better. This crystal is of violet shades. Deeper shades of violet are very good — for meditation as well.

15 ▸ Place a Pyramid on your desk or in your study area. The Pyramid is a powerful geometric shape and this helps the child concentrate on what is to be done.

The study table should be kept tidy and uncluttered — unlike the study table shown here

OTHER ROOMS — GUEST ROOM, SERVANT'S ROOM & GENERATOR ROOM

We tend to overlook the guest room, servant's room and generator room Vaastu-wise. There are Vaastu rules as to where the guest room should be located, and why. Vaastu also tells us about the placement of the servant's room so that the harmony of the household is not affected. Likewise, the generator, which has become a must now, needs a proper location. It emits a lot of noise, smoke and pollution, in addition to consuming a lot of electricity. All these factors combine to generate negative energies. Hence, the correct positioning of the generator room is essential for creating a positive Vaastu environment.

According to ancient Indian texts, the guest is a representative of God. We should take care of the total well-being of the guest, and the placement of the guest room should be such that the host benefits from the guest, and the latter too remains healthy. Domestic helps have been an integral part of the Indian culture since the Vedic period, perhaps even before. And whether we like it or not, they need their own space too. And then there is the placement of the generator room within the structure to think about. Just follow what Vaastu dictates, and you won't get confused about the location of these rooms.

GUEST ROOM

We Indians are a hospitable lot, and consider the arrival of a guest as auspicious for the household. While the guest does command total respect and care and attention, at the end of the day, the guest is a guest and should be treated accordingly. If we go through the Vaastu Shastra, we will find that this ancient text has laid down some rules and regulations that are to be followed in the location and other details of the guest room — which will ensure that both you and your guest enjoy each other's company and that the guest will return to his/her own home with sweet memories of his/her happy stay with your family.

1. The best room to be allocated as a guest room should be the North-west room of the house. This area represents the Air element, and does not provide stability in the structure. This will ensure that the guest does not become a permanent member in the family.

2. Under no circumstances should the guest bedroom be positioned in the South-west portion of the house.

3. Other areas such as the South-east and North-east are also not auspicious as far as the guest room is considered. The guest should not remain in the family and become a member of the (host's) family.

4. The guest room should have more openings, which should be towards the North and East wall.

5. The bed in the guest room should be aligned with the South wall of the room.

6. The guest room should be painted in white, violet, grey or light blue shades.

7 ▸ Make sure that any belongings or articles used by the host are not kept in the guest room.

8 ▸ Neither the master bedroom nor the kitchen should be visible from the guest room.

SERVANT'S ROOM

Nowadays we are, perhaps more than ever, even more dependant on servants for the smooth running of the household, what with a nuclear family in which both husband and wife work, leaving their children under the care of the servant/s.

In such a context, the servant's room gains importance as this is where the servant rests and restores his/her energy. Vaastu offers a few tips on the location of the servant's room.

1 ▸ The best location for the servant's room or quarter is on the West side of the house. This is because it is considered a neutral direction, neither strong nor weak. The North and East directions are very pious and pure, so a servant cannot be placed there. The South and South-west directions are very strong, so neither can the servant's room be located here as this means that he/she is sharing the Earth Luck with the person who is living in the South and South-west direction. This means, that the owner will be sharing his

Earth Luck with his servant, who will become dominating and stubborn if he/she is placed in the South-west.

2. If the servant's room is placed in the North-west corner of the building, they tend to leave the household early — which means that servants will keep coming and going, and the family will not benefit from a long and healthy association with the servant/s. This is because this area is not stable.

3. If the garage is located in the North-west, it can be converted into a room for the servant/s.

4. The servant/s should not be allowed to sleep in the kitchen.

5. The servant/s should not be given a room just above your bedroom. The servant will become a partner to your luck and try to gain an upper hand in the master–servant relationship.

GENERATOR ROOM

Thanks to recurring power cuts, generators have virtually become a necessity in our lives. A generator ensures a good night's sleep after a hard day's work, as well as providing a comfortable environ for children to study in, and ensures that we don't miss that particular match or programme that we'd been waiting to see so eagerly!

Since the generator releases vast quantities of negative energy, the location of the generator room is important so that these bad energies do not affect us and our daily lives.

1. The generator room should be placed in the South-east corner of the building. Since the South-east is termed as a Fire direction, keeping a generator in the South-east is like complementing this direction. If, by any chance, this corner is already occupied, the generator can also be placed in the South.

2. The emissions of smoke from the generator should be released only towards the South or South-east. The North and East directions are considered as positive energy directions, and one should keep these directions particularly clean and pure so that maximum benefit can be derived from these directions.

3. The generator room should be decorated in dark colours and shades of red. The negative and harsh energies are absorbed by the dark and red shades.

4. Generators kept in the South-western area of the building burn the positive energies which were provided by the North-eastern

directions. Fire and loud and noisy activities should not be there in the South-west. It may bring disrepute to the owner, adversely affecting both his name and fame.

5 ▸ An elevated platform should be created below the generator. This gives a smooth flow to the Earth's gravitational energies.

VAASTU IN THE WORKPLACE

What shape should your office be? And your workspace? Where do you put up that honorary degree? What is the best combo for professional success? Just turn the page to find out.

During earlier times, many small-time businessmen operated from their home, often in a room dedicated to the purpose. Today, however, as businesses have expanded and requirements changed, independent offices have become an indispensable and universal element of the business world. Moreover, with increasing competition in the commercial environment, it is imperative that the place of work is stable and filled with good luck.

SHAPE

The shape of your office matters a great deal and must ensure elemental harmony. Your room/cabin should be regular-shaped and well-defined. There should be neither any extensions nor any cut corners. The ideal shapes are perfect squares and rectangles.

PLACEMENT

1. According to Vaastu, it is highly beneficial to have an office in a public place rather than in lonely or isolated surroundings. The office should be set amid the hustle and bustle of crowd and traffic, and an office building that is surrounded by running roads is considered very prosperous.

2. Office buildings that face the North, North-east, or North-west are also considered very prosperous, as these directions are extremely auspicious: they always attract good luck and positive energies.

3. Beware of beams overhead; they cause unnecessary stress. Beams hidden under false ceilings are as bad. A door directly ahead of you is not auspicious. Doors and windows, even behind the table, invite betrayal. Sit against a solid wall.

4. If your workstation faces the North, keep your files and any electronic gadgets like computer, etc, on the left side of your table. However, if your workstation faces the East, make sure that the aforementioned office paraphernalia is kept on the right side of your table.

5. Don't place yourself in the centre of the room; choose a corner towards the South or West. On your left should be a closed area or wall.

6. Facing the North or East while working is very auspicious and makes you feel fresh. The North is owned by Kuber, Lord of Wealth, and is very beneficial for those in the trading business, while the East — the direction of sunrise and growth — is excellent for professionals and those in the service industry.

WORKTABLE

1. Work on a regular-shaped table, like a square or rectangle. Strangely-shaped tables are not auspicious. An ideal table is one that has four corners. The length and breadth of the table should not be more than 1:2. If the length of the table is more than this recommended portion, it may lead to confusion and delays.

2. While sitting or working at a table, keep the table's left heavier but not with pictures/idols of gods! Do not place idols or images of deities on your desk, as this is not considered respectful. Gods are supreme powers and their idols should be placed in an area that is separate from day-to-day articles.

3. Avoid eating food at your workstation/table. Any activity that is unrelated to work should not be undertaken at your table.

4. Do not read magazines or indulge in other forms of time-passing activities while sitting at your working table. The office area should be used only for money-making activities; reading and sleeping here creates negative energies. Don't put down your head on your desk for a power nap.

5. Keep your table clean and uncluttered. Goddess Lakshmi does not like untidiness; hence, cleanliness is a prerequisite for any place of business. Clutter is believed to be responsible for creating confusion and problems in the workplace. It may also create disharmony between colleagues.

LIGHTING, PICTURES, CREDENTIALS

1. You should have adequate lighting in your office. Professionals like doctors, architects and designers can have dim lights but people in marketing and trade should have bright white lighting.

2. Pictures of water cascades without mountains are prosperous, when hung on the North wall.

3. Pictures of successful people like kings and business tycoons are also beneficial. Credentials and achievements should be placed on the western walls.

VAASTU FOR OFFICE

While setting up your office, or designing an office, it is important to keep in mind some Vaastu necessities in addition to concepts pertaining to interior designing. This is because planning your interiors, at work or at home, can enhance the positive atmosphere of your inner spaces manifold.

These basic Vaastu guidelines can do wonders for your office...

1. Doors in commercial establishments and offices should be well-painted. Any irritating noises while opening or closing doors disturb positive energies. Doors that open and close automatically are also not good.

2. Keep all dustbins concealed. Never keep them next to the door.

3. Make sure that when a visitor enters the premises, he doesn't face a door. A main door facing another door causes energy to flow out. To conserve good energy, locate doors in a zigzag pattern; this also enables energy to reach all corners. Moreover, display beautiful flowers or images.

4. Do not install mirrors or mirror-like objects in front of the main door, as they repel positive energy.

5 ▸ The reception counter should be in the North, never in the South, South-east or South-west. It should not be very high or have a business logo. The counter-top should not feature reflective glass. A water body in the reception area is very auspicious; however, the water flow should not be towards the main door, as this signifies that wealth is going out of the premises.

6 ▸ The office reception should reflect the nature of the organization and its power. The company profile or logo should be placed on the southern wall, and the reception table should face the door at a diagonal angle. Decorate the reception with flowers to attract positive energies into the office, and offer sweets to visitors in order to create good relationships with the outside world.

7 ▸ Seating for guests/visitors should be along the western wall.

8 ▸ The northern wall should be lighter, compared to the southern walls. All closets and storages should be made on the southern walls. Magnetic energy flows from the South to the North. If the North is burdened, the flow gets affected but if the South is burdened, the energy stays within the premises. The northern walls should be painted in light pastels and have maximum windows and openings.

9 General office files should be stored on the western wall. Sensitive files related to legal issues and taxation matters should be stored in the North-eastern corner. Papers and files related to banking matters should be stored in the South-western corner. Apply *kesar* or a *kumkum tilak* on banking and account books.

10 The marketing staff should occupy the North-west. As this area is related to the Air element, salespeople will be motivated to move out of the office and into the field.

11 The accounts and administration staff should occupy the East, and also face the East while working. The East is a good direction to manipulate fund movement.

12 Cash lockers and safes should also be kept in the South-western corner of the office. This is a stable direction and cash placed here also remains stable.

13 The top management should occupy the South-west. The head of the office should occupy the South-western corner. This is a very strong direction, and will help him/her control and manage the entire staff and associates efficiently. The person sitting here can

dominate the entire staff. Salespeople and lower cadres should not be given this area.

14 ▸ Make sure that no member of the staff sits with their back to a window or door while working, as this is considered extremely inauspicious.

15 ▸ Washrooms should never be located along the eastern or northern walls, as they can create financial constraints, payment problems and low business turnover. Also, washrooms in the North-east can cause major losses.

VAASTU TIPS FOR BOSSES & BUSINESS

Constantly worried about subordinates disobeying or disliking you? Perhaps you pay them peanuts? Jokes apart, use Vaastu to win over disobedient employees! Make your workplace a harmonious place for yourself and your juniors.

True, we all face difficulties in our workplaces at some point or other in our lives, but if your problems are overwhelming you, or if your business is steadily declining — or if you dread going to office because of your juniors — it's time you turned to Vaastu. Vaastu Shastra lays down a few simple tips which may improve your days as The Boss!

POSITIONING

The North-western corner of your office should neither be burdened nor be elevated in comparison to the South-eastern corner. Moreover, if you have placed your people in the South-west, they will grow more powerful and will try to dominate you. Clashes between employer and employee will become frequent and a source of tension at the workplace.

RECOGNITION

You earn lots of money, you have a need to be recognized through your work, but something is hindering that. Check the kitchen in your house. Yes, the kitchen. If it is located in the South-west, it is harmful. Similarly, heat furnaces and electric generators kept in the South-west in an industry create bad effects. Fire in the South-western corner spoils your efforts and achievements, by burning the magnetic energy stored here.

UNSTABLE BUSINESS

Do you have a great marketing staff but are still not getting the right results? In spite of giving your very best, are you unable to seal deals? Just when you think you've got it, does a competitor carry away the business? Check which direction the marketing staff faces. If it is the South, they will certainly not be paid for their efforts. Make them sit towards the North, and see that they do not have any obstructions in front, such as walls or cabinets.

DISPUTES

Disputes cause major tension in workplaces, by hindering professional growth. Check if the North-east houses any fire-related or heat-generating equipment. This is a major cause of frequent labour disputes in industries and offices. Due to this, several business houses can also get embroiled in time-consuming legal disputes. Also check the water sources. Are your water borings or underground water tanks in the South-east of the plot? Remember, the South-east is the fireplace and its owner is Lord Agnidev. Since Fire and Water are anti-elements, there is not much wisdom in positioning water features in the house of Fire.

ACCIDENTS

Furnaces, heaters or ovens in the North-east of commercial establishments and factories give rise to labour accidents. Keep the Vaastu alive to avert such accidents.

LOANS AND DEBTS

Loans that are difficult to pay off cause huge problems. Blocking the North is a major reason for debts. Placing heavy furniture or closets along the North wall, cluttering up the North and not giving enough openings are all Vaastu defects. Moreover, if the building structure is elevated in the North, it creates a Vaastu defect. In floors above the ground floor, if the North is covered but the South is left vacant, that too is a Vaastu defect.

LOSSES

Analyse the floor slopes in your building and the type of activity/usage in the highly sensitive North-east direction. Never situate washrooms or fire-related areas like kitchens in the North-east. Neither should it be used to store heavy materials.

GROWTH

To achieve your targets, you should know the Vaastu rules for growth. Check the flow of subtle energies in your workplace. North Pole energies boost your environment, so create more openings in the North than in the South. The North is owned by Kuber, Lord of Wealth, so open it up and keep it light and uncluttered. If by any chance, you cannot have any openings in the North, then it should be lighter and lower than the South. Check the orientation of the management and senior staffers and, in case of retail, the placement of the cash counters and locker.

VAASTU-SMART BUSINESS

1. Don't ever take loans on a Tuesday. In fact, do the reverse — always try to repay loan instalments on a Tuesday.

2. If you are lending money to someone, do not lend it on a Wednesday, for there might be difficulties in reclaiming it.

3. If burdened by loans and business problems, place a picture of Lord Krishna playing the flute and flanked by Radha and a cow. It is said that Krishna's flute takes away all your problems. But just hanging a picture will not help. Also work hard to counter other shortcomings that may harm your business.

4. Apply a Swastika with turmeric powder on the main door. Always light a *diya* outside the main door in the evening.

5. Follow the proverb "Early to bed and early to rise makes a man healthy, wealthy and wise". Wake up with the sun; it helps you and your business to grow.

**See Appendix for case studies of workplaces/factories.*

HEIGHT, ELEVATION & STAIRS

The height of a building has a major impact on its Vaastu, and has been discussed extensively in Vaastu scriptures. A building's height also contributes significantly to its attractiveness and stature. Stairs play a major role as well, and are of great importance in Vaastu science. Energies filled with the forces of life climb the stairs of a house and make their way throughout its internal structure.

Before constructing your building or house, spare a moment to plan out the height of the structure vis-à-vis its width. Vaastu Shastra has very well-defined and clear-cut rules and regulations on the correct proportion of the height and elevation of buildings. Along with height and elevation, comes the location and shape of stairs, which influence, rather strongly, the flow of positive energy. Whether this much-needed energy will visit our house and accumulate therein depends on the seemingly humble stairs.

HEIGHT AND ELEVATION IN VAASTU

You must have noticed that large, imposing buildings always seem to have an identity of their own. Different heights of buildings have been characterized in Vaastu as follows:

1. A building whose height is equivalent to its width is said to possess medium Vaastu, ie, neither very good nor very bad.

2. A building whose height is one-fourth more than its width is said to possess good Vaastu, and brings peace in the lives of its residents.

3. A building whose height is one-and-a-half times more than its

width possesses perfect Vaastu. These structures provide prosperity to their occupants.

4. A building whose height is three-fourth more than its width is believed to possess excellent Vaastu.

5. A building whose height is double its width possesses superb Vaastu, as this proportion of height and width is considered the best in Vaastu. It brings overall health and prosperity to the structure's residents.

Note: The Vaastu effects as stated above are only in terms of the heights of the buildings.

In addition to a building's height, some other ways of ensuring good Vaastu for your structure are as follows:

1. The elevation of South-facing building should be very heavy, with lesser openings in the form of windows and doors. The construction should be done in the front portion in case of South-facing plots.

2. The elevation for North-facing houses and buildings should be very light. The maximum number of openings and doors should be

provided to ensure that the magnetic energy of the North Pole enters the building structure.

3 ▸ The elevation — here elevation means the exterior of the house — for West-facing structures should, again, be a little heavy as discussed for the South direction: less windows and doors. This can be made heavy by constructing heavy pillars, covering the area with the roof, planting bushes, shrubs, trees, as well as decorating with sculptures, and choosing darker shades of fabric or painting darker shades to create more heaviness.

4 ▸ The East represents growth and you should ensure that the maximum amount of sunlight is allowed to enter the structure from this side. The ultraviolet rays of the sun are essential for all living beings and also cleanse the building of its negative energies. As such, the East should be kept open and light; most of the structure's openings and doors should be provided in this direction.

STAIRS IN VAASTU

Some points to consider when constructing stairs are as follows:

1 ▸ The best location for stairs is in the South, South-west and North-

west sections of a house. Do not place stairs in the northern portion of a building.

2 The number of steps in a staircase should be always odd, ie, numbers like 5, 9, 11, 15, 21 and so on.

3 Do not hang any pictures of gods or goddesses at the beginning, middle or end of the staircase. The reason for this is that each level of the staircase is occupied by a human being's feet, and hence, is not a clean, pure or respectable place for a God. Neither should you hang pictures of any human being (family or friends) under the stairs, as this area is not considered stable.

4 Spiral staircases are not auspicious and should be avoided. This is because spiral staircases encircle the building and bind it with inauspicious energy.

5 The staircase should always proceed in a clockwise direction. Anti-clockwise stairs bring in bad energies as they signify that the time circle of the residents is moving in reverse.

6 Providing a door at the head of a staircase is considered propitious.

7 ▸ Avoid constructing stairs in front of the main gate of a house or building as then all the good luck and energy will climb up the stairs and will not enter or circulate in the lower portion of the building.

8 ▸ Do not build a bathroom or sitting area under the stairs. This is considered to be very unlucky. You can, however, create a storage space here.

9 ▸ Never position a kitchen under the stairs as this will burden the prosperity of the house and make it stagnant.

10 ▸ Similarly, avoid constructing a *mandir* or a meditation space under the stairs as there are too many burdens crossing over it.

LEVELS, SLOPES & RAINWATER

The location of the various rooms of the house, placement of furniture and lighting of incense and candles are not enough to ensure and maintain the flow of positive energy in your home, if basic requirements such as levels and slopes are incorrect. The different levels in a building and the direction of slopes plays an important role, too.

The levels and slopes of a building have a significant influence on its Vaastu, making it either positive or negative. Similarly, the flow of water and its direction can make a structure healthy or unhealthy. This is largely due to the immense power and energy generated by the Earth's gravitational and magnetic forces, which are integral elements of the Vaastu philosophy.

1 ▸ The level of the floor in a house should be lower in the North and higher in the South. This results in monetary growth and financial opportunities for the residents.

2 ▸ A raised floor in the East creates problems for the children in the house and destruction of reputation.

3 ▸ Raised levels in the South-east bring unexpected monetary gains.

4 ▸ If the level of the floor in the South-west is raised, it brings stability, power and confidence.

5 ▸ A higher floor level in the West provides support to the children of the family and encourages higher education.

6 ▸ A raised floor level in the North-east results in all kinds of problems for the building's occupants, and even possible ruin for the family.

7 ▸ If the level of the floor in the North is high, it has a negative impact on the family's finances.

8 ▸ A lower level floor in the South-east is very inauspicious and may not only lead to diseases, but even death. The fear of theft can also rise.

9 ▸ If the level of the floor in the South is low, it may bring depression, ill health and delays in each and every aspect of your life.

10 ▸ If the level of the floor in your building is lowest in the North-east, it is very fortunate. This brings in much wealth and good health for the family. It also promotes higher education.

11 ▸ A depressed floor in the central portion of the house can result in all sorts of stomach diseases and many other problems.

12 ▸ Slopes of water moving towards the North brings financial stability.

13 ▸ A slope of water heading towards the North-east offers overall prosperity to the family.

14 Slopes of water moving towards the East bless the residents of the house with fame and fortune.

15 If a slope of water is aimed towards the South, it may result in financial losses and wastage of money.

16 A slope of water heading towards the South-west causes depression and delays in various aspects of life.

17 If a slope of water moves towards the South-east, there will be unwanted fights and legal tensions.

18 The best and most auspicious directions for rainwater harvesting are the North, North-east and East.

Times Group Books
Peace
Tranquillity
Happiness
Harmony
and Joy
now in 288 pages
THE TIMES OF INDIA
TIMES WELLNESS GUIDE
THE TIMES OF INDIA
TIMES
WELLNESS
GUIDE
In association with
MOTHER DAIRY
Good Life Series
Rs.150 only
www.tgb.indiatimes.com | tgbsales@timesgroup.com

VAASTU & WATER TANKS

Early man had realized the importance of water, and had established settlements along riverbanks. Major civilizations that had flourished and are still read and studied today are ones that grew alongside a water source. In fact, the oldest cities in India that are still heavily populated today are those beside rivers. This is because water is recognized and given importance as a life-giver.

According to Vaastu, the correct harnessing of the five elements brings harmony and prosperity in life, and Water is one of these five elements. Thousands of years back, settlements flourished alongside riverbanks — developing a settlement near a river is not possible in this day and age. And yet, irrespective of whatever substitutes man has found for gifts of nature, man has not found any substitute for water, and we cannot survive without water for long. The only option is to contain and preserve water in overhead and underground tanks. Governed by Lord Varundev, Water is an extremely potent element and commands our respect. Incorrect placement of these tanks — including septic tanks — can lead to difficulties in life. Correct placement, on the other hand, will flood our lives with prosperity and abundance.

UNDERGROUND WATER TANKS

This is the major requirement where water is scarce and not supplied regularly. Underground water tanks are also required in the multi-storeyed flats and small colonies. Correct location of underground tanks is important. For instance, placing these water tanks in the South-west gives serious Vaastu defects and creates major problems to the inmates of the structure. The problems include depression and anxiety, sometimes by causes unknown.

1. Underground water tanks in the South-west takes away both earned income and savings. Expenses can come in any form, whether it is medical or some other loss. It also takes away the savings of the family.

2. Underground water tanks made in the South-east gives fire-related problems. These problems have the nature of Fire that leads to clashes in the family, resulting in unwanted fights and a bad name among relatives.

3. Taxation and legal problems also confront the inmates. Thefts can also occur in the building.

OVERHEAD WATER TANKS

These tanks are required for instant supply of water to the bathrooms and washrooms. These tanks should be placed in the South-western side of the building structure. Placing the overhead water tank in the South-west gives inmates their confidence and immediate completion of projects.

1. Placing the overhead water tanks in the North-east part of the building creates serious Vaastu defects. It may create unwanted problems and bring in mental and health problems.

2. Placing the overhead water tanks in the South-east may bring the same problems as stated in the underground placement of water tank in the South-east.

3. Placing the overhead tank over the kitchen may bring in financial burden to the family.

4. Placing the overhead water tank on the bedroom causes sleepless nights, tensions and health problems.

5. The overhead water tanks should only be placed above the bathrooms.

SEPTIC TANK

Though modernization has taken place in almost all cities and places, the sewerage line does not reach some places for some reason or the other. Farmhouses in the outskirts of cities are a good example where sewerage is not available. Industrial units in remote areas also need to arrange for disposal of wastes. Very big and deep tanks are erected to accumulate human waste. These tanks may be called septic tanks.

1. These tanks should be made in round shapes only.
2. If this tank is erected in the South-west, it will create problems like delays and depression to the inmates.
3. Septic tanks erected in the North-east cause severe accidents and diseases.
4. Tanks erected in the South-east causes fire-related problems.
5. Septic tanks should only be built in the North-western areas, which is the best location for disposal.

OIL TANKS

These tanks are used to store oil, which is needed in some industries, and is an important requirement.

1. The oil tanks should not be placed in the North-east.
2. These tanks should not be placed in the South-west either.
3. The oil tanks should be placed in the eastern side, moving towards the southern direction.

VAASTU
for better living

COLOURS

The impact of colours on every aspect of our life — emotional, intellectual, materialistic, physical and intuitive — is immeasurable. This is because every colour has specific properties and characteristics that influence our moods, behaviour and even lifestyle. During ancient times, learned men realized the significance of different colours, and associated them with corresponding planets, the seven major chakras *(energy centres) in our body, and seven days of the week. It is no surprise then that colours play a major role in the creation of a good Vaastu environment.*

It is a well-known fact that colours are basically vibrations of light. When white light hits an object, certain wavelengths (vibrations) are emitted, and these form different colours. White light can be divided into seven primary colours of the spectrum — red, orange, yellow, green, blue, indigo and violet. These colours can then be combined to create secondary colours and shades.

In order to bring harmony in our life and create a Vaastu-friendly environment, it is important to understand the properties of these primary colours. Read on.

Red: This is the colour of blood and has an obvious association with our life and body. Red is associated with the base *chakra* and symbolizes lust, passion, materialism and other base energies, as well as being associated with Fire. It provides activity, energy and will power.

1. The façade of structures facing the South direction should be painted red; those who do not like red can add a red colour element to the front exterior. Inside the structure, you can paint the South wall of the living room red to create life-force energy.

2. Rosy red or pink shades can be used in the bedroom as they

symbolize deep love. Pink is an ideal colour for newly weds, and should especially be used by couples wishing to conceive. People who are generally irritable or couples facing conflict in their relationship can also benefit by this colour. In fact, pink can be used anywhere in the house.

3 ▸ Deep or dark red shades signify anger and should not be used in bedrooms.

Orange: This colour represents pride, ambition and communication. It also signifies health and vitality.

1 ▸ Young, aspiring people who are yet to achieve their goals in life should use orange shades on the southern wall of their bedroom.

2 ▸ Since orange is a fiery colour, it should not be used by people who are angry by nature.

3 ▸ Orange shades can be used in kitchens that are located in the South or South-east.

4 ▸ This colour also signifies an increase in life; hence people who feel low should use orange shades frequently. You can use orange in

the puja room as this is an auspicious colour.

5 ▸ Orange is associated with the *Sacral Chakra*, which is related to the excretion systems, genitals, bladder, pancreas and kidneys. Therefore, people experiencing such problems should incorporate the use of orange in their life.

Yellow: This colour signifies illumination, light, intellect and higher mental activities. It is also a colour which finds approval with Goddess Lakshmi. Yellow is good for studies, concentration and stabilizing the mind, and is best suited on the northern walls of a building.

1 ▸ Structures that face the North should decorate their front with yellow colours, thereby attracting and inviting in Goddess Lakshmi. Similarly, rooms positioned in the northern section of a house should have yellow colours.

2 ▸ Since yellow has a cementing and firming nature, people with fractures and weak bones should wear clothes of this colour.

3 ▸ Yellow is the colour for the solar plexus *chakra*, and those with behavioral problems should use this colour, as it would help them.

4. This colour is also considered to be very good for prosperity. Yellow semi-precious and precious stones can be kept in cash boxes or wallets to encourage the inflow of wealth.

Green: This colour symbolizes nature, fertility, abundance, prosperity and the growth of positive energy. It also represents rebirth, signifying the re-creation of new ideas. Green is a healing colour as well, and also has a cooling effect on persons with an irritable, stubborn nature.

1. Green can be used as a remedy by couples experiencing clashes in their married life; pastel green shades in South-eastern bedrooms have a soothing effect. This colour is connected to the heart *chakra*. Hence, it is good for heart and high blood pressure problems.

2. Green is a harmonious colour for the East, and structures facing this direction must have an element of green in the façade. Consultants, architects, designers, fashion stylists, and others in the consulting profession should have a green element in their office.

Blue: This is the colour of the sky, and also represents Water. It signifies emotions, inspiration, devotion and truth. Blue is also a healing and merciful colour, and helps reduce pains in the body. This colour is associated with the throat *chakra*.

1. This colour can be used in children's bedroom. However, it should not be used in a kitchen, restaurant, office or a shop, as blue is a reducing colour and has an unstable nature.

2. The most harmonious direction for using blue is the West. This is because Varundev, Lord of Water, owns the West and blue represents Water.

3. Its use is strictly prohibited in the South-east as this direction signifies Fire, which is in complete contrast to Water, represented by blue.

Indigo: This colour offers a deep connection to the inner self, creates spiritual qualities, and enhances psychic abilities.

1. It can be used anywhere, except in bathrooms and kitchens. However, it is ideal for meditation and study rooms.

2. Using white or yellow with violet makes for a positive combination.

3. Indigo is the colour of Lord Krishna, and hence, is very auspicious to use.

Three exciting ways of looking at a holiday home

Excellent Real Estate Appreciation!

Assured Rental Returns Every Month!

A Lifetime of Holidays - anywhere, anytime!

4. This colour relates to the brow *chakra*, and affects the eyes, ears and face. As such, it enhances the faculties of clairvoyance and intuition.

Violet: This colour represents religious devotion, knowledge and temperance. It enhances spiritualism, improves memory and concentration, and provides stability of mind.

1. Violet is best used in puja and study rooms, and is ideal for students, scholars and people whose work requires a lot of mental activity.
2. Violet should not be used in bathrooms and kitchens.
3. If used in great quantities, violet brings in spirituality. Therefore, in places that are filled with ambitions and a materialistic approach of life, such as business and trading centres, usage of violet should be restricted.
4. The colour also offers contentment in life. As such, people who feel dissatisfied all the time without any reason should use more of violet. This colour is also good for people who are indecisive.
5. Violet relates to the crown *chakra*, and controls the nervous system.

TIPS FOR A BETTER LIFE

To enjoy a good life, there should be a balance in all aspects of our lives, be it the spiritual or the physical and one should neither forget the natural world surrounding us. Vaastu too is all about harmony and can help us attain a happy balance in our lives by allowing positive energy (or thoughts) flow in our homes. Since it is not always possible to go in for major reconstructions, simple Vaastu guidelines may be followed to bring the harmony back in our environment and life.

In situations where, due to various predetermined factors, an unbalanced Vaastu has already created an environment of disharmony, it is difficult to prevent or put a stop to the generation of negative energies, but we should try to at least clean and rid the house or structure of its negative energies. Keeping areas, especially corners, clean and free of clutter, using a positive combination of colours for décor, playing soothing music, and lighting pure sandalwood incense are some of the many helpful techniques that can be used to clean the negative energy of a building.

TIPS RELATED TO THE SPIRITUAL WORLD

APPLYING TILAK

In Hindu society, the *tilak* is applied to invoke a sense of purity and stability in the wearer. The same holds true for a house or any other building as well. Before applying the *tilak* on your building, it is necessary to locate the centre of the structure from the front. The height should be 6–8ft from ground level. This will be the forehead of the building, and a *tilak* placed at this point augurs prosperity. A *tilak* should also be applied on the main door and all other doors of the structure, except the bathroom doors, above the wooden *chowkat* of the door.

The properties and colour of the *tilak* should be decided based upon the requirements of the building's residents. For instance, if one is seeking peace and tranquility, a white sandal *tilak* should be applied. If there is a lack of ambition, vigour and aggressiveness, a red *kumkum* powder *tilak* should be applied. Those wishing to attract wealth and financial prosperity should apply a yellow saffron or turmeric powder *tilak*, while those seeking control and command should apply a *bhasma tilak*. The latter also eliminates negative energies from the structure. In order to gain more power and increase prosperity, *tilaks* should be applied in the shape of symbols such as a Swastika or an Aum. A u-shaped *tilak* is used to symbolize the feet of Lord Vishnu, the Preserver in the Hindu Trinity. Adding rice to a *tilak* not only enhances its beauty but also attracts prosperity and fulfilment of food and many luxuries.

DEMON FACES

Many people believe that hanging a demon face outside their house helps ward off the effects of *buri nazar* (evil eyes) and negative energies. However, this is not true. The presence of a demon face anywhere in a building is considered inauspicious, as only beautiful and pious things can usher in good luck and prosperity. Hence, it is preferable to draw holy symbols on a structure.

Some people place pictures of deities outside their house. This should also be avoided, as it is not very respectful to the gods. In a sense, we leave them outside, unprotected from the harsh sun, rain, dust and storms, while we sit inside, enjoying the comfort and luxuries of the house!

SPIRITUALITY

Even after all requirements are met, you must thank the Almighty. Make your environment healthy. Use violet shades to enhance the spirituality in your environment. Press your index finger and thumb together for some time to concentrate on your karma.

TIPS RELATED TO THE PHYSICAL WORLD

BODY POSTURES

Some people have a tendency to sit crossed legs or cross their arms across their chest. Both these positions are unreceptive in nature and not welcoming. People using these postures frequently are usually stubborn and poor recipients of the good things in life. Adopting an open posture with legs and arms is preferable and more beneficial. A straight posture helps in the free flow of energy from the base of the spine to the rest of the body.

HEALTH

If you are not healthy, you cannot work hard and flourish. Do not position a bathroom in the North-east of your home — it leads to chronic diseases. If a couple uses a bedroom in the North-east, they may have problems in pregnancy, leading to abnormal children. Never place your head towards the North when sleeping — the North Pole's magnetic energy will disturb your sleep. Toilets, underground water tanks and swimming pools in the South-west also jeopardize health. A bedroom in the South-east may lead to high blood pressure and irritability. The East side of your plot, where the sun rises, is sensitive. Never block it, or you may experience eye-related problems, strokes, paralysis and severe headaches or migraines.

FIRE

Fire is one of the five sacred elements and should never be touched by one's feet. This includes items such as matchsticks and cigarettes, which are connected to Fire and hence should not be snuffed out with one's feet. Neither should you use your feet to push open doors. Rubbing your feet against each other also brings bad luck, and try not to sleep with your legs crossed. Goddess Lakshmi blesses people who keep their feet clean and odour free.

GOOD LIFE PARTNER

The right partner makes your life journey simpler by cushioning you from all the jolts involved. To find the right partner, apply the law of equality. Wherever there is darkness, balance it out with light; wherever there is dullness, provide sharpness. Strike balance between male and female energies, between receiving and giving. Combine colours and sounds well.

RESTLESS MOVEMENTS

Unnecessary and fidgety movements of hands and feet are considered inauspicious. For instance, tapping or drumming on tables or on parts of your body in idle fun or as a pastime should be avoided.

DAILY BATH

One should bathe on a daily basis. This keeps negative energies at bay. Bathing with sea salt also gives a tremendous boost to the flow of positive energies.

STUDYING

While studying, make sure that there is a solid wall behind you. The presence of a window or any opening facing your back does not provide any energy support and results in lack of concentration. Also, make sure that your study area is free of clutter such as old mails, notes, non-working pens, junk stationery items, etc.

DINING

During earlier times, people used to have their meals in the kitchen. This activity was and is still considered very auspicious for the residents of a house. One should face the North while eating meals. It is also beneficial to offer the first portion of the food to the stove (the Fire) itself, another portion to a cow and subsequently to a dog. You can even donate food to organizations that take care of street cows and stray dogs. These offerings are very helpful in clearing the effects of any previously earned bad karma.

PARENT–CHILD RELATIONSHIP

Ego strings attached to this relation can create bad vibes. If the North side of your building is higher than the South, it may be an uncomfortable relationship. If the son occupies the plot's South-west, he will try and dominate the relationship, perhaps even clash with the father.

SECURITY FROM ENEMIES

This indicates a secure life where you have no enemies in your life. Scan the South-east of your structure for main entrances and water sources.

TIPS RELATED TO THE MATERIAL WORLD

GOOD INCOME

Never say "I am poor". This way you increase your problems and worries. Always give dues and balances on time. Facing the North opens up opportunities for making money. Check the water slope in the house; it should not face the South or South-west. Boost the North Pole energy by clearing obstructions from North to South. Enter the house from prosperous directions and beautify the entrance points. The doors should have no obstructions inside or outside. Let time be in your favour — place wall clocks and calendars in the North.

LIGHTING

Darkness within a house or any building symbolizes dullness, depression and tension. Every evening, switch on all the lights of your house, even if it's for a short period of time. This helps vanquish the essence of darkness. Furthermore, the North-east corner of your house should be kept lit at all times.

POSITIVE SOUNDS

It is very auspicious to ring bells in all corners of a house. The sound of ringing bells helps vanquish negative elements, even many types of bacteria! The sound made by a *shankh* (conch) is also believed to be very powerful in ridding the house of all negativity. Playing light and soothing music also promotes healthy and positive vibes.

NAME AND FAME

It is important that you gain these in society. Money cannot bring you name and fame, but the reverse is true. Enhance your East direction by keeping it clean and beautifying it; never burden it.

HOUSE CLEANING TOOLS

Brooms, mops and other house cleaning equipments should not be kept under the staircase. Keeping dirty or soiled things under the stairs creates Vaastu imbalances. These items should also not be kept in the North, North-east and East directions of the house as these directions are very pious. Furthermore, do not keep the brooms standing, and avoid touching them with your feet, as this is very inauspicious.

TIME AND DATE ARTICLES

Objects such as wall clocks, timepieces and calendars should not be hung on walls that are located in the South, South-eastern and South-western directions. This induces an unfavourable time phase in one's life. Clocks and calendars should also not be placed above doors. Another important thing to note is that all the clocks in the house or office should be in working condition. If they are not operational, wrap them in paper or place them in a box and store them in a cupboard.

MONEY

If the flow of money in your life seems to be stagnant, it means that the energies in your house are stagnant. Providing ventilation in the house, ringing bells in all corners, and increasing the use of multi-coloured lights will help these energies flow smoothly and improve your money situation.

NAILS

Hammering nails into the walls in order to hang decorations and paintings should be avoided, as this hurts the walls. Use brass screws for hanging objects on walls.

FRONT COURTYARDS AND WALLS

Ensure that the front courtyard or any sections of it in a house or office is not broken or worn out. There should also be no clutter in this area. Ignoring these aspects could result in tensions for the building's residents. A damaged front wall that is broken or has peeling plaster is also inauspicious, and can increase the chances of litigations and government problems. All the walls should be intact and well-maintained, much the same way we take care of our clothes.

TIPS RELATED TO THE NATURAL WORLD

ESSENTIAL OILS AND INCENSE

Incense and essential oils of flowers are pious and have cleansing properties, and as such help enhance the positive energies in the environment. Light and burn them regularly to clear the house of negative energy forms.

PETS AND PLANTS

Taking care of all living things, including animals and plants, is very auspicious. As such, keeping pets — dogs, cats, fish, horses and others — brings good luck. Feeding birds and insects is also considered very positive. These activities heal our karma and help take away some of our problems. Plants and trees are also living beings, and maintaining them means maintaining your own life. You can also create a favourable Vaastu environment by feeding animals and pets from your kitchen, and watering plants from your own water resources. When these life forms share your food, they also share your sorrows, hence reducing your burdens.

REJUVENATED ENVIRONMENT

A great way to re-energize and breathe fresh life into your room is by adding elements of nature such as fresh flowers to it. Lighting candles, burning aromatic incense sticks, playing light music and decorating the room with some happy pictures is also beneficial.

CRYSTALS

These semi-precious stones are famous for their amazing cleansing properties, and are a very powerful tool in cleaning negative energies. All quartz crystals work as a filter for various energies and have six primary properties — they are able to structure, store, amplify, focus, transmit and transform energies, including those related to matter, thought, emotion and information. Crystals naturally harmonize and energize our gross (physical) and subtle (the energy circle or aura surrounding us) bodies.

Crystals have many uses and can be used in many ways.

1. A crystal elixir can be made by placing some crystals in a bowl of water for a few days. This water can then be sprinkled within a building to clean the negative energies present. This elixir can also be used for drinking, as crystals have healing powers for many diseases. These rocks come in different shapes, sizes and colours,

and may carry different properties that can be used to heal different problems in life.

2 ▸ Crystal rocks can be kept in rooms to absorb the negative energies released by the people living there. Keeping crystal rocks can clean feelings of depression and diseased energies.

3 ▸ You can also wear crystal pendants and strings. However, these should be used according to the healing properties of the crystal. For instance, rose quartz crystals offer soothing energies and reduce feelings of anger, irritation and grudges in relationships.

4 ▸ Some crystals are carved in a variety of shapes, such as balls, stars, pyramids, etc. Each of these shapes can be used as healing tools for a range of ailments, and to create or divert a person's subtle energies so that it wipes out any Vaastu defects.

VAASTU FOR HAPPINESS

Secret to inner happiness?

Giving creates abundance. The more you give, the more you receive. An example from nature: you cannot keep inhaling air; you must exhale too.

In which aspect of your life are you experiencing scarcity? If you lack love, first give love unconditionally. And then see it grow all around you. If you feel a cash crunch, let it flow from you first. Give out regularly from your income — whatever you can afford — and it will return, ten times over. Never give pain and hatred. Sustained hatred and grudges manifest themselves as serious diseases in your physical body. Lighting an oil lamp outside your main door is a very auspicious ritual in Vedic Vaastu. It brings light into your life.

LAW OF ACCEPTANCE

This is vital for happiness. Accept everything as it comes. You cannot change the seasons or the cycle of day and night. One who stays calm, whether in moments of ecstasy or anguish, is a perfect human being.

LIFE-FORCE ENERGIES

The universe is full of subtle life-force energies like North Pole energy, magnetic energy, gravitational energy and solar energy. When you build your home or office, ensure an obstacle-free flow for these. And if the structure is already built, and built incorrectly according to Vaastu, you must attempt to purge the negative energies: keep the area clutter-free, play good music, light sandalwood incense, and mop the floors with sea salt in water.

PETS AND PLANTS

Keeping pets like dogs, fish and horses is very good Vaastu. Feeding birds and insects is also auspicious. It heals our karma and takes away some problems. Plants and trees need to be nourished and nurtured. Maintaining plants is like maintaining your life. Trees and animals share your food and resources, and your sorrows as well.

FIVE ELEMENTS

Our body is made of five elements: Earth, Space, Fire, Water, Air. Earth gives shape and smell to our body, Space produces sound, Fire gives thirst and hunger, Water supports blood and other fluids and Air gives the feeling of touch. If there is complete harmony among all five elements, the body will remain healthy. The human body is a structure for the soul to live in, just like your house is a place for you to live in. Your house must be built to maintain elemental harmony.

BODY VAASTU

The Vaastu factor applies to the human body as well. Our body postures hold immense importance. Sitting with legs and hands crossed at the chest level is not a receiving posture. Legs and arms should be in open positions. Moving and shuffling hands and feet without any reason is also inauspicious. It is good to face the North when working or eating and point one's head to the South when sleeping.

VAASTU FOR ENERGY — HOW TO TACKLE LOVE, LIFE OR LACK OF BOTH

Everyone lacks something. Or thinks he does. Of course, there are no limits to what a person wants and craves. But, if some basic needs are not fulfilled, life can be very tough.

There comes a point in our lives when in spite of working hard, things don't seem to be working out the way we had hoped, and dreams die gradually. In addition to this, we go that extra mile, when building our houses, to follow the Vaastu dos and don'ts, so that life, at least at the personal front, will be smooth. But it doesn't, and we feel discouraged as something is missing, making our lives incomplete. Vaastu tells us what to do, and how to go about it.

LACK OF CONCENTRATION

Concentration is a potent tool for success, be it in studies or career. Family stresses hinder concentration and create problems at work. Some of our body energy centres (*chakras*) are also responsible for mental stability and concentration. Increased use of yellow and violet colours helps concentration. See that you always face the North while doing mentally-exhausting work. Also, there should be open space in front of you. In case you cannot arrange these, place a pyramid in front of you.

LACK OF RECOGNITION

You earn lots of money, but do people know you? You crave recognition by society but something is not right. People don't acknowledge your achievements. Check your kitchen. A kitchen in the South-west direction is considered extremely inauspicious according to Vaastu. Ovens, boilers, heat furnaces and generators kept in the South-west area of a factory or plant have adverse effects. As the magnetic energy stored here gets burned, the Fire in the South-west reduces all the hard work, planning and strategizing that you had put in.

LACK OF ENERGY

You eat well, you earn well, you are fit… so why do you lack life-force energy? Why do you feel fatigued and lethargic at times? Bring red and orange into your life. Your root *chakra* (energy based at the spine end), responsible for basic energy and transmutation to the higher *chakras*, may be depleted. If the energy line (starting from your home's North-east corner and going to the South-west) is broken by any excavation, energy will dissipate. Similar effects will be felt if the magnetic energy line is burdened by any pillar or heavy furniture.

LACK OF HAPPINESS

Do you feel good in one place but uncomfortable in another? This is due to subtle environmental energies, both negative and positive. Consider a hospital and a religious place. Everybody comes to a hospital with problems; though the hospital relieves problems, it is a depressing environment. People come to a religious place with problems too, but the environment is soothing. Why not enhance your environment through Vaastu? Sleep with your head pointing towards the South. Do up your place in a pleasing combination of light and dark colours. Place an amethyst quartz crystal in your living area for calmness. In office, always sit against a solid wall, not a window or door. Also, avoid sitting under a beam — it generates stress.

This festive season, feel lighter and happier. Check out your home for negative energies. They obstruct good health, good relations, good careers. Identify them and remove them! Eliminate all clutter.

IDENTIFYING NEGATIVE ENERGIES

IRRITATING NOISES

Creaking doors and windows kill the positive energy resident in your home. Oil the hinges to stop the creaking. Noises made by moving furniture around are not good either.

BATHROOMS AND KITCHENS

Subtle energies get contaminated when bathrooms are placed at their source points. Similarly, they get burnt and depleted when kitchen and other Fire activities are positioned at their sources.

CLUTTER

It is difficult to get work done and really relax amid clutter. It adds to stress and builds negative energy. It also drains your physical, mental and emotional strength. In Vaastu terms, clutter is "stuck-up energy". To identify clutter, ask yourself whether the object is operational and/or beautiful. If you get two "no", well, what are you waiting for — de-clutter now! Anything that you have not used for a long time should also go; don't hang on to articles that you haven't used in recent times, thinking that you'll need it sometime in the future.

DEAD THINGS

Non-functional wall clocks and disused electronic gadgets signify dead and negative energies. Clear these at once. Dried flowers in vases also create negativity. Replace them rightaway.

DEPRESSED MOODS

When you are depressed, you exude negative energies, which get accumulated in your home. Then, even when you are not depressed, this bank makes you low.

DISEASED ENVIRONMENT

If someone in the family is ill, the diseased energy is shed in the house and the entire environment gets dull.

PURGING NEGATIVE ENERGIES

ESSENTIAL OILS AND INCENSE

Aromatherapy candles, incense and essential oils of flowers have cleansing properties. They encourage the flow of positivity by refreshing our senses, and uplifting our moods which in turn lead to happy and progressive thoughts. Light and burn them on a daily basis to reduce and remove negative energy forms and thoughts.

LIGHTING

Darkness is the symbol of dullness, depression and tension. Once in the evening, even for a brief period, all the lights of the house should be switched on. It makes the essence of darkness vanish. The North-east corner should always be illuminated.

SOUNDS

Ring bells in all corners of the house. This pealing eliminates many types of bacteria. Conch sounds are also very powerful in clearing negativity.

SEA SALT

Sea salt can extract negativity. Place some sea salt in bowls in every room, also under a sick person's bed. This salt has to be changed periodically, approximately every 15 days. You can also use sea salt in water to mop the floors, as it cleanses the environment.

NATURE

Sunlight coming into your home cleanses the negative environment. Proper transmutation of sunlight creates a salubrious environment.

CRYSTALS

This is the most powerful method to clean up negative energies. These are semi-precious stones extracted from the Earth. The quartz family is particularly powerful and will eliminate negative energies, thereby enabling the flow of positive energies.

WEEKLY
NOTES
ADDRESS
FORM
AUGUST
6 JUNE
9 SEPTEMBER
12 DECEMBER

VAASTU FOR LIFESTYLE

A better lifestyle is what we all seek, and we all strive to that end by working hard. But a bit more than that is needed; a positive outlook does wonders as it leads to positive energies. So go ahead, bring that zing back into your life!

Your happiness rearranges your fortunes to bring you even more joy. Avoid fear, anger and frustration at all times. Feel good about yourself and others. Feel the happiness in your heart and transmute it into a smile. Improve your lifestyle, clothing, and food to improve your fortune...

ENHANCE POSITIVE ENERGIES

Create strong positive energy in your house/office structure. Good illumination, de-cluttering and soothing combinations of sharp colours enhance strong energies.

ELIMINATE NEGATIVE ENERGIES

Igniting pure sandalwood incense makes for a cleansing effect. Using sea salt in the water used to mop floors and keeping some sea salt in a bowl near you extracts negative energies.

USE THE NORTH

Maximize the use of the North direction. Face North while working to be blessed by Kuber, Lord of Wealth. By eating and drinking when facing the North, you will be energized by the North Pole energy. Sleeping with your feet pointed to the North ensures good health.

BLOCK THE WEST

Try to close the West direction as much as possible. Openings in the form of doors and windows should be avoided towards the West. Such openings drain away your money and your efforts.

AVOID IRREGULAR SHAPES

Vaastu recommends four corners in any plot, building structure or room. More than four corners create a Vaastu defect and plots with more than four corners should be avoided. L-shaped plots are a severe Vaastu defect. Rooms which have their corners cut give the effect of five or six corners but create a Vaastu defect. Architectural creations to beautify such multi-cornered rooms should be avoided, as they hinder proper distribution of energies.

TIPS FOR SUCCESS

CREATE STRONG ENERGIES

Create a strong energy environment around you. Good lighting, de-cluttering, maintaining cleanliness and using soothing colours in combination with sharp colours are some steps to achieve this.

NO OBSTRUCTION

Let energy flow freely in front of you. Never work on a table pushed up against a wall. This obstructs energy from flowing towards you. Making a big bookshelf on the table also hampers energy flow.

USE OF FINGERS

Hands and fingers carry all the energy of our bodies. All the five elements are available on our fingers. Don't rotate or move your fingers needlessly; such actions drain the body of energy.

POSTURES OF THE BODY

Always sit upright and erect. This is a smart and correct posture. It helps in the free flow of energy from the base of the spine to all parts of the body.

IDENTIFY THE NORTH-EAST

Decorate the North-east corner of your home and office. Put up colourful lights and fresh, fragrant flowers. Include a Water element like a fountain here to further strengthen the North-east and boost prosperity.

POINT TO THE SOUTH

Always point your head towards the South when sleeping. This assures sound and healthy sleep. Since electromagnetic waves revolve from North to South, pointing the head towards the North makes one vulnerable to the waves coming from the North, leading to aches and pains in the morning.

APPENDIX

CASE STUDY 1 — WORKPLACE/FACTORY

BACKGROUND

I was invited to a tile and ceramics manufacturing unit in Khurja district, a place which is famous for ceramic products. Every division was working in full capacity, and the production unit in question was especially export-oriented. Its speciality lay in creating unusual designs.

However, the unit was plagued by a number of labour accidents, as frequent as once in three months, and all accidents were fire-related. Fortunately, there were no casualties.

The other major problem they were facing was rejection of orders, in spite of manufacturing quality ceramic products. Another problem was with the owner himself. He was so busy attending to his business clients and other small business-oriented jobs, that he hardly had any time to sit at his factory office. Further, whenever he came to his factory, anxiety and depression filled his mind.

ANALYSIS

The factory was not in a regular shape. The North-east corner was not in a right angle — a Vaastu offence. The magnetic energy from the North-east was thus distracted, creating problems like accidents in the factory.

CORRECTIONS

- The regular shape of the factory was the first and foremost requirement. A rectangular-shaped energy grid was created with pyramids made in precious stones, and quartz crystal powder was put along the lines of the energy grid.

- The energy grid also helped to "bring back" the missing right angle in all the directions, including the powerful and important North-east direction.

- I advised that the North-east must be made the cleanest and neatest area in the unit.

- The North-east corner was beautified with a water fountain, and highlighted with a spotlight.

- The North-east corner was painted a lemon-yellow colour.

RESULT

- The number of accidents virtually stopped. A feeling of satisfaction came upon the staff, and the labourers were eager and willing to work. Business increased, as did the number of satisfied clients.

- The owner became focused at his work and was able to give his full concentration to the matter at hand.

CASE STUDY 2 — RESIDENCE

BACKGROUND

I was invited to a residential house of a big businessman in Meerut. The family was facing problems and delays in each and every project that they undertook; unnecessary and unwanted tensions too existed. Moreover, their daughter's marriage was getting delayed. The 30,000sq yard-bungalow was architecturally a beauty, both impressive and majestic. Although Meerut is quite a crowded town, the bungalow stood in the outskirts of the city.

ANALYSIS

- On making an external analysis, I found the bungalow to be West-facing, with a beautiful open area in front. But open areas in the West-facing direction are not considered Vaastu-friendly.

- The gate of the bungalow was situated in the South-west, which is a serious Vaastu defect. The South-west is owned by a demon and if a gate is constructed here, the residents of the building/bungalow will be prone to innumerable problems. This defect may create countless delays, too, in one's life.

- A gate in the South-west meant that the driveway was automatically created in the South, thereby keeping the southern direction open in the bungalow, which is again another Vaastu defect. The South should be closed and heavy in comparison to the North. The floor level was lower as well. This defect may cause anxiety and depression, severe financial crisis and may bring suicidal feelings to the occupants of the house.

- On moving inside, I saw that the master bedroom was in the South-west; thankfully, the architect was aware that master bedrooms should be in the South-west. But again, the problem here was the position of the bed: it was positioned towards the North.

- In the bedroom, one corner had been extended as a round-shaped sit-out; this disfigured the room and was yet another Vaastu defect.

- One of the bedrooms was in the North-east, and was occupied by the businessman's daughter. Her marriage was getting delayed and her health too was not good — this room should not have been made a bedroom.

- The kitchen was placed in the northern direction. The North is an energy direction and ensures a good flow of finances. The kitchen in the North burns the financial energy.

CORRECTIONS

- To negate the bad vibrations from the West, I advised them to plant heavy trees on the western boundary, and a rockery without water on the West wall, towards the South to make this direction heavy.

- To avoid energy leakage from the South-west and to stop the bad energies of the demon from entering the bungalow, I advised them to set up a very heavy metal gate and to paint the gate a dark shade.

- To create weight in the South driveway, I suggested that heavy plants be put on South walls. Further, they should paint the South boundary walls in red to absorb the energies of the North.

- Change the direction of the bed from the North to the South.

- All rooms with a rounded extension had to be changed into a rectangular room, either by getting it redesigned or by putting up a false wall.

- Regarding the daughter's room which was in the North-east, I advised them to turn it into the study room and shift her bedroom to the North-west side, as this might increase her chances of getting married.

- A kitchen in the North can be termed as a destroyer of finances; painting the kitchen a shade of lemon was one advise, the other involved shifting the gas stove to the South-eastern side of the kitchen, facing the East side.

RESULTS

- The efforts proved fruitful, and the family was able to successfully complete whatever project they undertook; therefore, tensions arising from delays lessened and eventually vanished.

- Their daughter got married very easily into a good family.

- Their business grew fast and flourished, and consequently the family earned both name and fame.

CASE STUDY 3 — RESIDENCE

BACKGROUND

I was invited by one of my old clients to his brother-in-law's — a high-class business family — house. They owned 4-5 industries. Three years ago, they had married their youngest son to a healthy and beautiful girl; the problem came in the second year of their marriage. The youngest bride of the family started having miscarriages, and the son remained in depression almost all the time.

ANALYSIS

- On visiting their home, I checked out the stores, bathrooms, elevations, kitchen and the bedrooms of the family members, although the problem mostly centred around the youngest couple.

- After visiting their bedroom, I realized that the bedroom was in the North-eastern corner of the plot and it had a combined bathroom too. A bedroom in the North-east is a literal defect in Vaastu. This is a place for Lord Shiva and a generation point for magnetic energies. Hence, this place is considered very pious and one should not have a bedroom in this corner. The energies generated from this area also harm us when we are asleep: this was the main reason for her miscarriages.

- Now the other biggest problem was the North-east bathroom. A bathroom in this place makes scope for accidents and surgeries, and this is what was happening in the family.

CORRECTION

- I strongly suggested that the couple's bedroom be shifted. The family had a guest room bang in the West direction, which often lay vacant; I told them to shift to the western rooms.

- I also advised them to point their heads towards the South, and paint the room white.

RESULT

- With time, life blossomed in the family. The couple was blessed with a healthy baby girl.

- The emotional and physical health of the couple too improved.

- Prosperity and abundance came to the family.

CASE STUDY 4 — RESIDENCE

BACKGROUND

This is about one of my very good clients; I had visited his factory once. He invited me to his house. He was extremely worried about his married life. His wife was a professional working in a multinational company, and they had two small children — a wonderful, loving family. None could imagine that this couple had any differences. The main problem was the severe and frequent clashes between them; sometimes they even ended up hitting each other.

ANALYSIS

- After analysing the whole structure, I found that the bedroom was in the South-eastern corner of the house. The entire southern area was open with big windows and a door which opened onto a beautiful lawn. From the bed one could see gurgling water run towards the South. From this direction, the head pointed towards the North.

- The South-east is dedicated to the Fire element and owned by Lord Agnidev. Having a bedroom in the South-east means having a bed above a fire! This was the reason for the sudden fits of anger in either partner, and the cause of their fights.

- Having a water body in the South also provokes the Fire element and subsequently, stokes anger.

- Pointing the head towards the North meant that neither the husband nor the wife slept peacefully at night.

All these combined factors resulted in the couple frequently quarrelling and fighting with each other.

CORRECTION

- The family had no option but to shift their bedroom. I advised them to put up a wall in the South, and shift their bed towards the South.

- I also suggested that the room be painted either pink or pastel green.

RESULT

- Gradually their (sudden) anger reduced, and subsequently came down to manageable margins.

- The relationship between the husband and wife improved and became more stable.

CASE STUDY 5 — RESIDENCE

BACKGROUND

This is one of the most interesting cases that I have faced in my career. I was called by a well-settled family to visit their daughter's home. She had been married one-and-a-half years ago to a famous doctor in the city. The problem quoted to me was that the doctor's career had not yet taken-off; in spite of being quite renowned, he did not have a regular, stable income from his hospital. The other problem, the girl felt, was that her husband had a roving eye.

ANALYSIS

I visited their home and particularly checked out the couple's bedroom.

- The bedroom lay in the North-west direction of the plot. This direction is owned by Lord Vayudev, and hence not considered stable as it is basically a Wind element corner. This corner bedroom is not suitable as a master bedroom. Business suffers, and the grounding factor remains missing from this corner.

- Instead of having a single double bed, there were two single beds, which, of course, were joined together. The doctor-husband was fond of fish so he had placed a big aquarium on the South wall of the bedroom.

All these defects created an emotional distance between the couple — there was no love left between them, and both partners were busy finding faults with the other, blaming each other, and complaining against one another.

CORRECTION

- I advised them to shift the master bedroom to the South-west instead of the North-west.

- To redo the bedroom and bring in some charm and feminine energy to the bedroom. Pink and bright shades were suggested, colourful pictures of birds and greenery was suggested. A romancing picture of Lord Krishna with Radha was suggested on the front wall of the bed.

- A single bed was suggested with a single mattress to bring harmony in their married life.

- To remove the aquarium from the bedroom and place it in the drawing room, which lay in the North-east corner of the plot.

RESULTS

- The profits of the hospital increased in a significant volume, and the number of patients availing the hospital facilities increased.

- A feeling of confidence came to the doctor. His income became regular, which gave security to his wife, who grew more relaxed and cheerful. With this came a change in her attitude towards her husband, and she grew more attentive and caring towards him. Consequently, the strained relationship that had existed between the couple gave way to an improved and loving relationship.

CASE STUDY 6 — KITCHEN

BACKGROUND

This is a middle-class family, with just four members — a husband and wife, and their two children. The husband had a touring job, with the usual salary package, while his wife remained at home to take care of both the house and their children. The family was satisfied in terms of finance and relations. The only major issue for the family was the housewife's health problems — she had had two major operations in the span of five years.

ANALYSIS

- The house was East-facing, and the owner knew that this was a good direction as he had heard from his grandfather that the East was good for prosperity, as the sun rose from this direction every morning. They were totally satisfied that their house was Vaastu-friendly as it was East-facing. Within the house, the *mandir* and the drawing room were in the South-east; the dining room was in the East; and the kitchen was in the North-east.

- The North-east is the source point of energy, and if this energy is not properly utilized for circulation in the house, Vaastu defects may arise. The Vaastu reason behind the lady's poor health was the location of the kitchen in the North-eastern part of the house. All other room positions were fine and had no adverse effects on health.

CORRECTIONS

- Shift the kitchen to the South-east corner of the house, which is the Fire place and the position of Lord Agnidev.

- As a remedial measure, I advised them to paint the kitchen lemon yellow; this colour releases more energy.

- To keep a quartz rock under the gas stove.

- To burn camphor on the aroma lamp in the kitchen.

RESULT

After carrying out my suggestions, the lady's health improved tremendously. The family grew in confidence and stability. Their faith in Vaastu grew strong.

CASE STUDY 7 — KITCHEN

BACKGROUND

This is about a joint family of three brothers, all engaged in running their father's business in Sadar Bazaar. All of them were married, and with children. The family members enjoyed good relations with one another, with no major conflicts amongst themselves. Their unity started crumbling after they renovated their house two years back and differences arose among their wives as well. The family was on the verge of breaking up.

ANALYSIS

- After a visit, I realized that except for the kitchen — which was located in the eastern part of the house — the placement of the other rooms and bathroom was acceptable under Vaastu. Kitchens located in the eastern part of the house drain away peaceful energies.

- There was another severe defect: the gas stove and the water sink were not in the right position. The gas stove was placed in the North wall and all Water arrangements were to its right. Firstly, there should not be any Fire in the North wall and secondly, there should be no Water element on the right-hand side of Fire.

Both are anti-elements and clashed with each other, providing the perfect environment for disagreements within the family members!

CORRECTIONS

- To paint the kitchen a pastel leaf green shade.
- Shift the gas stove to the eastern shelf wall, and water connections to the North wall.

RESULT

Some level of satisfaction returned among the members and the feeling of irritation lessened, thereby enabling them to live peacefully once again.

CASE STUDY 8 — BEDROOM

BACKGROUND

This is the case history of a businessman — an exporter — who lived with his family in DLF City, Gurgaon. At that time, he was facing problems in his business, as well as having a difficult time in taking simple decisions. Moreover, he and his wife were both suffering from breathing problems.

Although this businessman did not believe in alternative sciences, including Vaastu, he called me for a consultation on somebody's referral. However, I don't think he believed that this would help or make a difference in his circumstances.

ANALYSIS

- When I visited him, I asked to be taken around the whole house. It was a beautiful house: the front faced the South, and the entire façade had big windows and openings that overlooked a lovely lawn. Based on my understanding of this layout, I informed the businessman that he was probably going through big losses in his business, had little savings, that his business was possibly going downhill, and people were, in all likelihood, getting dissatisfied with the services and products that he was offering. The businessman agreed that this was an accurate reading of his current business situation.

- Among other Vaastu defects, one was in the positioning of the main gate, which was located in the South-west corner of the house. I asked the businessman whether he had been facing major delays in collecting payments from his clients, and he instantly agreed. This was because the magnetic energy, which emanates from the North-east and stays in the South-west, was leaking through the opening provided here. As a result, there was no energy left to support the house, causing delays and a decline in business.

- Inside the house, I noticed that the master bedroom was in the North-west direction. This corner belongs to the element of Air, and this was the reason for the man's instability in business and state of indecision.

- The attached bathroom was in the exact North-west corner of the house.

CORRECTIONS

- Shut down some South-facing windows in the front of the house, and use heavy shutters, blinds or curtains on the windows that could not be closed permanently.

- To place heavy furniture near the walls in the South. This would stop the leakage of positive energy emanating from the North, and help the South remain cool.

- To plant tall trees in the lawn, also located in the South, as this would help keep the lawn dense and dark, and save it from the harsh energies of the sun.

- Regarding the position of the main gate, I advised him to shift the main gate a little off to the South-eastern side. If this wasn't possible, then he should construct a heavy metal gate in the South-eastern corner so that there is weight in that area. I also advised him to install a smaller gate within the main gate so that the larger gate could be kept closed at all times.

- To shift his room to the South-west corner in order to stabilize his business and improve his confidence.

- Remove the bathroom from the North-west corner, as this would improve his health and relieve him and his wife of their breathing problems.

RESULTS

- Gradually, in a few weeks after the changes advised by me had been incorporated, the family began to notice the improvements taking place in their life. Their health problems started disappearing, which lead to a reduction in related medical expenses.

- The businessman also experienced a miraculous change in his financial dealings — payments started coming in regularly and his clients began approaching him for more business.

- The members of the family became more confident and started thinking positively, bringing about a complete change in the total attitude of the family and their lifestyle, a fact acknowledged by the businessman himself.

CASE STUDY 9 — BEDROOM

BACKGROUND

This is the case of a well-to-do family in Vasant Vihar. They had a well-settled family business, running successfully for the last 50–60 years. Mr Gupta, his wife, their three sons and one daughter made up the family. As the head of the house, Mr Gupta occupied the South-west room and was respected by the entire family. His three sons were obedient and hard-working. All four male members of the family were in good health. The family was, however, facing great difficulty in finding a life partner for their daughter. In spite of their best efforts, they were unable to find a good match, even though the girl was highly educated and very presentable.

Another lesser-known problem was the severe depression that Mrs Gupta was experiencing. She suffered from anxiety and was not very sociable. As a high-status family, they were invited to several parties, but Mrs Gupta had no interest in these get-togethers. Although both husband and wife did not communicate much with each other, their relationship could still be called harmonious, and there were no disagreements in the family. However, Mrs Gupta felt that something was missing in her life.

ANALYSIS

- The first thing that I noticed when I visited their house was the swimming pool in the South-west corner. Although this pool was not very big, its presence was significant enough to cause delays in the daughter's marriage. The South-west direction represents the Earth element, and the swimming pool, symbolizing the

Water element, was taking away the Earth element from that place. This resulted in a leakage of the magnetic energies emanating from the North-east corner of the plot. The depression and feelings of sadness that Mrs Gupta experienced was also due to the location of this swimming pool. As the men in the family remained outside the house for most of the day, they were less affected.

- I was also concerned about the couple's sleeping arrangements. Their bed was positioned correctly, with the head facing the South. While Mr Gupta pointed his head towards the South when sleeping, Mrs Gupta slept pointing her head in the opposite direction, the North, which is very inauspicious. This was also one of the reasons for her depression. Moreover, the door of the bathroom was located just behind Mrs Gupta's head.

CORRECTIONS

- To remove the swimming pool.

- I also asked Mrs Gupta to sleep with her head pointed towards the South, and to change the position of the bed slightly so that neither the feet nor the head point towards the bathroom door.

RESULTS

- Following my suggestions and the changes that the family carried out, Mrs Gupta began to feel much better and became quite confident and relaxed. She also started taking greater interest in socializing and get-togethers.

- The relationship between the couple also became quite comfortable, as compared to the slightly strained feelings they had been experiencing earlier.

- Soonafter, Mr Gupta's unmarried daughter got married into a nice family, without any difficulties.

CASE STUDY 10 — BATHROOM/WASHROOM

BACKGROUND

This case study is about a husband, wife and their two children, one son and one daughter — a very compact family. While the husband ran a factory, his wife was a home-maker. The son was 14-years-old and the daughter was 19-years-old.

The major problems that the family faced were serious health issues. The head of the family had a kidney failure and had undergone a transplant, but it wasn't successful, and the transplant failed after a year. The son had a hole in his heart — a problem since birth. The daughter suffered from serious depression, and was always sad, while the mother, a housewife, was very bold and spiritual, and had faith in God.

ANALYSIS

- The house was West-facing, and the entire structure was more or less Vaastu-friendly.

- The bedrooms were in the right direction; the kitchen was in the South-east.

- All the bathrooms were in areas/directions as advised by Vaastu. I was surprised to see such a Vaastu-friendly house reeling from such severe health problems.

- Finally, as I completed checking the interior and stepped out in the back courtyard, I found a big, elevated bathroom in the extreme North-east corner of the plot. This was the only Vaastu reason for so many health problems in the family. The North-east is the purest and sacred point in a plot. This place is owned by Lord Shiva and is the direction from which energy starts its flow. This is a severe Vaastu defect.

CORRECTION

There was no other option but to demolish the bathroom. I strongly urged them to immediately pull down the bathroom.

RESULTS

The family agreed to my suggestion for the sake of betterment. The results were amazing.

- The second kidney transplant was successful.
- A surgery rectified the hole in the son's heart.
- The daughter started managing her father's business and subsequently her depression vanished.

CASE STUDY 11 — BATHROOM/WASHROOM

BACKGROUND

I was called by a business house, which had various business interests, one of which was a restaurant in a very crowded area. This restaurant was quite popular and a profitable cash-generating unit.

In spite of the restaurant's popularity, the owner faced a lot of flak from his customers who were dissatisfied and complained volubly about the quality of the food and service rendered by the staff. The management was honest in serving the customers but could not avoid clashes between the staff and the guests.

ANALYSIS

- The restaurant was North-facing. The sitting area of the clients was in the North and the North-west area, and the western area was covered.

- The cash counter was in the South-west corner, which was correct Vaastu-wise.

- The raw material was also in the South-western area which too was right. The kitchen was in the South direction, which was fine.

- Then I analysed the South-east corner, which had a block of washrooms — visitors' washrooms, staff washroom and workers' washroom. The washing area for the kitchen was also in the South-east corner.

- This was the only Vaastu reason for the oh-so-many complaints to the restaurant management. The South-east is dedicated to the Fire element, the position of Agnidev, Lord of Fire, and placing a washroom in this corner disrespects Lord Agnidev. The Fire element in this area was troubled by the Water element — the water used in the kitchen and washrooms. The element of Fire is a sensitive element and should not be disturbed. This was a severe Vaastu defect.

CORRECTION

Demolishing the washroom was the only option, and I strongly suggested it.

RESULTS

- There was a huge transformation in the attitude of the clients.

- The appreciation and the goodwill of the restaurant increased.

- The standard of quality maintained was already high but the confidence and appreciation gained by the management prompted them to go for other changes in the restaurant and its income increased manifold.